Praise for
HUSBANDS, WIVES AND SEX

"Doris Wild Helmering's new book is on target and straight as an arrow. Nobody can quarrel seriously with her contention that while both partners contribute to the problems, one partner, alone, can be effective in breaking the logjam and beginning the process of resolution. On top of that, the book is a good read, holding our attention as it broadens our horizons."

Darrell Sifford, Philadelphia Inquirer
Syndicated columnist and author of The Only Child

"*Husbands, Wives and Sex* puts forth real people, recognizable models, that help an individual analyze his or her own marriage. What I like most is that the author doesn't offer simplistic, mechanistic advice. Rather, she shows that our heads, hearts, and lives all activate or suppress our sexual appetites. Doris Helmering focuses our attention on how to create an environment where sex can be satisfying and frequent."

Pepper Schwartz, Ph. D. Professor, University of Washington
Co-author, American Couples

"If your sex life isn't all that you had hoped for, this book will give you a better psychological understanding of why it happened, what the power struggles are, and how to go about making repairs."

Penny Wise Budoff, M.D.
Author, No More Hot Flashes and Other Good News
Women's Medical Center, Bethpage, Long Island

"THE book for every man and woman in recovery who desires sexual and emotional intimacy."

Mary L. Boeger
National Council on Alcoholism and Drug Dependence

"When a relationship is in trouble, the first thing to disappear is intimacy. Doris' book is the first step toward getting it back. Whether you are a hopeful romantic or a hopeless romantic, if you want to keep the relationship spark alive, I recommend this book."

Robert J. Ackerman
Co-founder, National Association for Children of Alcoholics
Author, Perfect Daughters

DORIS WILD HELMERING

Husbands Wives & Sex

How one partner <u>alone</u> can change the dynamics to renew sex, romance and intimacy

BOB ADAMS, INC.

ISBN: 1-55850-009-X

Published by Bob Adams, Inc.
260 Center Street, Holbrook Massachusetts, 02343

Printed in the United States of America.

J   I   H   G   F   E   D   C   B   A

This publication is designed to provide accurate information with regard to the subject matter covered. It is not, and is not intended to be, a substitute for consultation with a qualified physician. if medical or other expert assistance is required, the services of a competent professional person should be sought.

The names used in this book are not the actual names of the persons interviewed. These names are fictitious.

To Skeeter
  My Special Friend
  . . . with love

To Serra
  My Noble Pal

CONTENTS

Foreword by Virginia Johnson Masters

FOREWORD

This is a well-organized and very readable book.

It has been thirty-two years since I first joined the ranks of those referred to as pioneers in the field of human sexuality and set out, with Dr. William Masters, to find ways to help people overcome problems related to sexual function and intimacy. The ultimate goal was to develop enough scientific knowledge with which to educate the "world" in ways which would prevent sex-related problems from ever occurring. Such idealism provides inspiration for commitment and hard work, but fortunately it must give way to reality. This reality seems to be that each person must encounter and identify their own unique problems before they seriously consider new information.

The result of work in the field is a reasonable body of material relating to sexual function and behavior and a range of methods of counseling and psychotherapy from which health care professionals now draw in treating those who come to them for help.

But people who seek help from professional sources represent only a small percentage of the population. Doris Helmering addresses the great number of individuals and couples who need to be able to resolve their sexual concerns or distress on their own initiative. They haven't the time, the money, or even the need to take their problems to a psychologist, marriage counselor, or sex therapist. They may not even recognize the nature of their need or realize that help exists until a book such as this gives them the insight and the reassurance.

Many will find themselves and their particular situation reflected in Ms. Helmering's sometimes humorous, always to-the-point accounts of situations and types of behavior which lead to pitfalls in an intimate relationship. In the context of circumstances and people drawn from her extensive professional experience, she offers an opportunity for understanding to those who are trying to find answers to their own problems.

In my opinion, Doris Helmering has written a women's book. But where better could a man look to find information and insight into his partner's feelings and needs. Doris has especially important contributions to make to those women who have entered marriage without skills in sexual communication or who are without a clear sense of how to blend and balance their own ideas, needs, and preferences with those of their partner.

In fact, this is not just a woman's book. It is a book for couples who care for one another and want a mutually satisfying sexual relationship.

Virginia Johnson Masters
Masters & Johnson Institute
St. Louis, Missouri

ACKNOWLEDGMENTS

It's fall in St. Louis. The leaves are turning. I hear acorns dropping on our roof. The birds are squawking and chattering in the woods outside my window. Earlier this morning I made final corrections to this book. I have just finished typing the dedication page. And now comes the time when I get to say "thank you" to the many people who gave me help and encouragement while I was writing.

I thank each of you who came to my office—once, twice, sometimes three times—to share the intimate details of your relationship and your sex life so that others might gain insight into their own lives. Although I did not include everyone's story, and I know some of you will feel disappointed when you find your story was not included, each of your stories was genuinely valuable. Collectively, they helped me put the puzzle pieces together, to better understand the factors that consistently interfere with a couple's sex life. I will always treasure the time I spent interviewing you, laughing with you, and at times sharing a cry.

I thank Dr. Hugh Ritter, Dr. Richard Mackey, Jane Kniestedt, and the Edgewood people, who all found couples for me to interview.

Skeeter, once again you were Mr. Wonderful while I wrote this book. Thanks for the hand holding, the hot coffee, and the many hugs and pats on the back.

Serra Bording-Jones, you've lived with me through the writing of another book! Thanks for listening and listening some more.

Anna Mary, thank you for all the snacks and ice water you brought me while I was sitting at the computer. I still have those "I love you" notes that you left me on my tray.

April Oppliger, how many times do you think you listened to your Sis read you this manuscript over the telephone—long distance no less! Maybe five times? You are the best!

Germaine Eley, thanks for always being available when I needed to check out a paragraph or a test, or when I just needed a friend.

Thanks, Mom and Dad, for your pats on the back.

John and Paul, thanks for all those long-distance calls and queries, particularly, "How's it going, Mom?"

Martha Scharff, thank you for your friendship, belief in me, and ongoing support. Nifty lady!

Kathy Meder, thanks for the many readings and encouragement. Lelia Anne Jones, thank you for reading my work and giving me good feedback when I needed an emotional boost. It meant a lot.

Judy Cassidy, you are a neat woman. Thank you for all the encouragement while I was writing this book, and thanks for your skillful pruning and tightening of the manuscript. Phil Rheinecker, thanks for your editing help and quick turn-around time. "A whole manuscript in one day?"

Pat Gross, thanks for taking such good care of me.

I also want to thank all the excellent therapists in our office who led the therapy groups when I was out writing. Thanks to Pat Cannon, Michaeleen Cradock, Mary Sue Wofford, Ann Weisman, and Anne Brooks. You are all excellent therapists, and besides that I love you.

Linda McKay, how many times did you make changes and print the manuscript? Thanks for all your "hurry-up-we've-got-to-get-this-out-today" help. Also, thank you, Lisa DiTiberio, for transcribing the interviews.

Richard Rennecamp and the people at Westgate, Caryl Avery, Dave Gosnell, Bill Bolster, and everyone at Bob Adams, thanks for your quick response on November 7. We came up with a new title!

You're all terrific people. Thank you!

CHAPTER ONE

HOW YOUR MATE'S PERSONALITY
AFFECTS YOUR SEX LIFE

"We feel like everyone else in America has more sex than we have," says thirty-five-year-old Lisa. "We might have sex once a month, but sometimes we don't have sex for six or seven weeks. If we haven't had sex in a long time, there is an awkwardness there, like, what should we do first?"

"We have sex about every three weeks," says Anne, "although we may not have sex for six weeks at a time. I think it's because I'm always angry at Tom. Tom always does what he damn well pleases."

"Sex," says George. "It's not a high priority with me, and Toni is pretty shy about sex. Actually, we're both kind of shy. Neither of us talks about it. If we do talk about it, it is in the context of her criticizing me for not being more sexually active."

In this book you will read intimate interviews, in which men and women tell about their sex lives. You will learn how often they make love, who does the approaching, and how the issue of power is connected to who initiates sex and who refuses it. You will learn in what ways men and women think differently about marriage, and why they often feel misunderstood and dissatisfied with each other. Most important, you will come to see that men and women have very different personality types, and that this dramatically affects their sex lives.

You will take four short tests later in this chapter to determine your own personality type and the personality type of your mate. As you take these tests, you will begin to see more clearly how your personality and that of your mate affects your sex life. And you will come to understand that infrequent sex is almost always the result of an underlying unhappiness with one's mate that begins outside the bedroom.

?&· WHAT MEN COMPLAIN ABOUT, WHAT WOMEN RESENT

Contrasting the most common complaints that men and women bring to marriage counselors gives some real understanding of why spouses often feel so misunderstood— and eventually alienated from each other sexually.

A man's most frequent complaint by far is that his wife is too critical of him. He feels angry and resentful because he never seems to be able to please her. Moreover, her criticisms are hurtful and not easily dismissed or forgotten.

Another common complaint of many a husband is that his wife does not appreciate what he actually does in the relationship. Instead she constantly focuses on what he doesn't do.

Men also complain that women always seem to want to talk and analyze and dissect the relationship. And in this dissecting it is the man who gets a lecture and becomes the bad guy.

Many men want sex in the morning, when their testosterone level is 30 to 35 percent higher than at night. Most women feel they must get the chores done before it is okay to relax and have sex. Therefore, a woman is more likely to want sex in the evening.

In addition, many men report that they feel closer to their partners after sex. Also, the actual act of sex is frequently a man's way of feeling emotionally intimate. Women want to feel emotionally close *before* they have sex. Talking and sharing is often a woman's way of feeling emotionally intimate.

Most men have their emotional needs consistently met by their wives, because their wives make them the center of attention. It is rare, therefore, that a man will focus on the marriage and think about what needs to be changed or how it might be improved. Most women's intimacy needs, on the other hand, are not met by their husbands, and as a consequence it is typically the woman who is always trying to improve and fine-tune the marriage. In order to get some perspective on how much women focus on relationships compared to men, all one has to do is compare the number of women's magazines that contain articles on How To Improve Your Relationship to the number of men's magazines that contain such articles.

A woman's most frequent complaint is that her husband does not take care of her emotionally. She does not feel she is the center of his attention or that she is a high priority in his life. She complains that her husband doesn't talk to her, or put his arm around her, or tell her he loves her. Nor does he make her feel special. He does not take her wants and needs into account before he makes a decision to do something.

The wife further complains that she is the one who does most of the chores around the house. And she is the one who does most of the emotional caretaking. For example, if her husband comes home in a bad mood, she tries to make him feel better. She talks with him, asks him questions, and tries to help him solve his problem. She may even offer to fix him a snack or give him a backrub. But if she comes home in a bad mood, he probably won't notice. And if she takes the risk and tells him about her bad day, he is likely to dismiss her with a quick "band-aid" comment such as, "It will all work out; you'll see."

Women also complain that their husbands frequently do not do what they say they will do. Instead, they do what they darn well please.

Another large group of women complain that their husbands are too passive. Although they are nice guys, they lack motivation, do not make decisions, and don't take responsibility in the relationship.

ॐ THE DYNAMICS THAT STOP SEX

Looking at but a few of the dynamics that underlie these complaints, it's easy to see that if a man doesn't do what he says he's going to do, his wife is going to be critical. The more he doesn't do what he says he's going to do, the more critical she becomes. The more critical she becomes, the more he does what he darn well pleases. And soon, neither is approaching the other for sex.

Her justification for avoiding sex is that she's hurt and angry because he doesn't do what he says he will do. His justification is that he's hurt and angry because she's always nagging and complaining.

As one man said, "I don't approach her more because of her anger. I say to myself, 'She's too angry.' I would rather go to sleep than to try to talk through what's bothering her so we can have sex."

Here is another dynamic that frequently halts sex. The wife complains to her husband that he does not pay attention to her. At the same time, she continues to give him attention and do nice things for him. What this wife fails to realize is that, by continuing to take care of her husband when he does not give her what she wants, she inadvertently supports his nonattentive behavior.

As one woman so aptly put it,

"Throughout our marriage he never saw how important caretaking was. I think it's because he was never without it himself. He didn't see that I, too, needed taking care of. If you are always being taken care of, you never feel the void yourself. You can't see that the other person in the marriage might be suffering from a lack of attention."

In addition, even though a wife's complaint about her husband's lack of attention may be legitimate, her husband is likely to feel annoyed and put off by her complaining. As a result, he gives her even less attention, and he is not likely to want to make love.

Another far-too-familiar dynamic that keeps couples out of the bedroom: he tries to be helpful and she criticizes.

For example, the husband starts fixing breakfast. He's not very adept, though, because he hasn't done it as often as his wife. The wife, watching her husband's ineptness, jumps in and starts flipping the pancakes. Consequently, this husband now does less—and the wife does more.

As the wife stands at the stove, she starts to feel put upon, becomes critical, and wonders why her husband can't do anything right. The husband feels criticized and caught in a damned-if-I-do, damned-if-I-don't position. Both partners feel misunderstood—and sex becomes less and less frequent.

ઢ MEN AND WOMEN BEHAVE DIFFERENTLY IN RELATIONSHIPS

After years of working with both men and women in therapy and closely watching the dynamics that occur between the sexes, I came to recognize four very distinct personality types. The four types are Caretaker, Corrector, Passive Aggressive, and Passive Taker.

Most women tend to fall into the category of either Caretaker or Corrector. The Caretaker's main focus in life is taking care of others. The Corrector's main focus is pointing out everyone's flaws and telling others what they should and shouldn't do.

Most men, on the other hand, tend to fall into the category of Passive Aggressive or Passive Taker. The Passive Aggressive's main focus is himself. He is the man who pretty much does what he pleases. The Passive Taker has no focus. He is willing to go along with whatever his mate decides, but he rarely takes the lead or makes decisions in the marriage.

When you look at these four personality types in detail, you will understand why you behave as you do, why your mate acts as he does, and how your sex life is directly affected.

&. THE CARETAKER WOMAN

The Caretaker sees her main job as taking care of others, both physically and emotionally. She can walk into a room and instantly know what her mate is feeling. If he is down in the dumps or angry, she immediately goes into action and tries to make him feel better. It's almost as though her happiness depends on his happiness.

If Caretaker and her husband are driving and he mentions that the car sounds as though it needs a tune-up, she starts figuring out when she can take the car to the shop. What's interesting is that her husband has not asked her to get the car repaired, nor does he expect her to do it. She, however, expects this of herself. Caretaker is also the woman who watches Monday night football with her husband, even though she hates football, because she thinks he needs the company.

Caretaker is too concerned with her mate's happiness; she loves too hard and does too much. In many ways a Caretaker's life tends to be what William James called "Zerrissenheit," meaning "torn-to-pieces-hood."

The Caretaker Test

To determine if you are a Caretaker, take the following test. Check off each item that applies to you. Or take the test with your partner in mind.

1. Caretaker is constantly concerned about her mate's mood, is forever taking his emotional temperature, and feels responsible for his feelings.

2. Caretaker gives compliments, hugs, pats on the back, and presents, and she always tries to please.

3. Caretaker may or may not approach her husband sexually, she may or may not demand orgasm for herself, but she believes it is her job to help her mate achieve orgasm.

4. Caretaker prepares well in advance for birthdays, holidays, vacations, and social gatherings so everything will be just right.

5. Caretaker is willing to drop her own plans for those of her mate at a moment's notice.

6. Caretaker has a high energy level, she is ambitious, and she is a doer.

7. Caretaker has the ability to look at a situation and recognize instantly what should be done.

8. Caretaker has trouble relaxing, and when she does, she still works on little projects such as paying the bills while watching television or wiping off the kitchen cabinets while talking to a friend on the telephone.

9. Caretaker is well organized, efficient, and somewhat compulsive.

10. Caretaker secretly enjoys taking charge and making sure things get done.

What's Your Score?

If you have checked off eight, nine, or ten items, you or your mate is definitely a Caretaker. If you have checked off five, six, or seven items, you are not a die-hard Caretaker, but your score indicates that you still put others' needs first most of the time.

She Won't Approach Him for Sex and She Won't Respond

In the beginning of the relationship, a Caretaker is most concerned with pleasing her husband emotionally and sexually. As one Caretaker woman said, "When the relationship began, I would get pleasure out of giving pleasure to Marc."

After a while, however, Caretaker starts to expect to be taken care of in the same way that she takes care of her mate. When this doesn't happen—and it won't, because he thinks differently than she does—Caretaker starts to feel angry and discounted.

In response to these feelings of anger and disappointment, Caretaker rejects her husband's sexual advances. She reasons, "Why should I do what he wants when he doesn't consider me?" And she refuses to approach him for sex.

🐛 THE CORRECTOR WOMAN

The Corrector is the woman who thinks there is a right way to fold socks, hang towels, put toilet paper on the holder, and have sex. And she is more than happy to tell her partner "the right way" to do something.

One man who is married to a Corrector said, "She criticizes the way I hang my ties in the closet. She criticizes the way I have my drawers organized. If my shoes look dull, she says, 'You never shine your shoes.' I was getting ready to walk out the door this morning and she says, 'Why are you wearing that coat with a crease down the back of it?' She drives me crazy with her comments. How can I possibly want to make love to her when she is always on me about something?"

Another man speaking of his Corrector wife said, "Every time we have sex, it's like she's grading me. She says, 'It was great' or 'It was so-so.' If I lose my erection, she says, 'What's wrong with you?' I had my T-shirt on the other night when we were making love. Instead of her romantically taking it off, she says, 'Will you take that damn T-shirt off?'"

The Corrector Test

Now let's see if you are a Corrector. Take the following test and check off each characteristic that applies to you. Or take the test with your mate in mind.

1. Corrector is overly critical of herself for things she did or didn't do. She mentally reviews her performance.

2. Corrector is overly critical of her partner and quick to point out his flaws. Off the top of her head, she could easily name a number of tasks her partner does wrong.

3. Corrector continually strives to be perfect and considers herself a perfectionist.

4. Corrector tends to define the world in terms of black and white, right and wrong, good and bad. Her thinking is often polarized. Once she has made a decision, she has trouble understanding or accepting the other person's point of view.

5. Corrector frequently does not approach her mate sexually and often turns him down because she is irritated with his behavior.

6. Corrector uses anger in various forms—sarcasm, guilt, pouting and not talking, temper tantrums and

put-downs—to intimidate and control her mate and to get her own way.

7. Corrector enjoys telling her mate what to do, and she gets a feeling of satisfaction when she explains how to do something.

8. Corrector schedules free-time activities carefully to get the most out of her time and rarely engages in spontaneous play. Her fun usually has a purpose. As a result, she often sees having sex as a task to be accomplished and checked off her list of things to do.

9. Corrector is well organized and efficient and gets a lot done both at work and at home.

10. Corrector thinks of herself as someone who can be counted on, is loyal, and keeps her word.

What's Your Score?

If eight or more of these characteristics apply, you or your mate is definitely a Corrector. If five, six, or seven characteristics apply, you are still guilty of correcting too much.

He Won't Approach and Neither Will She

As time passes, it becomes increasingly difficult for a man to want to make love to a woman who is always correcting and lecturing and pointing out his flaws.

Perhaps one man put it best when he confessed, "It's hard to make love to someone who thinks that badly of you, even if she's right. Over the years I've become more and more insecure. I also think that if she has such a low opinion of me, she's not going to find me sexually attractive, so I don't approach her very much."

And over time the Corrector finds it more and more difficult to see her mate's good qualities and to feel loving and sexual toward him, because she is so focused on his flaws.

ಐ THE PASSIVE AGGRESSIVE MAN

The Passive Aggressive man operates from an I-count-more-than-you-count position, which translates into behaviors that constantly discount his wife. Passive Aggressive does what he wants to do, when he wants to do it. He follows his own standards of behavior, as opposed to following the standards that others follow. Because he does what he wants to do, he is often late, he procrastinates, he forgets, and he frequently tells you he will do something and then doesn't.

Here's an example. Passive Aggressive suggests to his wife that it might be fun to "mess around" because the kids are spending the night at Grandma's house. His wife responds, "Sounds good to me. I'll meet you in bed in ten minutes." She then goes upstairs, showers, puts on dusting powder, and jumps in bed, where she waits . . . and waits . . . and waits.

Finally she yells downstairs, "What's keeping you?" Passive Aggressive yells back, "There's the best movie on. You ought to come down here and watch it with me."

By changing his mind and deciding to watch the movie instead of making love, and by not discussing it with his wife, this man implies that his wife is not important and that he counts more than she counts. This is aggressive behavior.

At the same time, this husband does not raise his voice or name-call; nor is he sarcastic. He simply changes his mind and keeps her waiting. His aggressive behavior is expressed passively.

The Passive Aggressive Test

If you think you are living with a Passive Aggressive, or if you believe that you might be one yourself, take the following test. Check off each item that applies to you or to your mate.

1. Passive Aggressive does what he wants to do, when he wants to do it, and how he wants to do it. He follows his own standards of behavior and often does not abide by the rules that others follow. In sex, he runs the gamut from very sensitive to very insensitive, depending on what pleases him.

2. Passive Aggressive resists others' expectations by dawdling, procrastinating, and "forgetting." He hates it when others set deadlines for him and frequently does not meet them.

3. Passive Aggressive gets angry when crossed. He has a nasty temper and often uses it to try to intimidate, control, and get his way.

4. Passive Aggressive thinks that others have no right to tell him what to do. When told what to do, he often responds in a defensive and hostile manner.

5. Passive Aggressive repeatedly does not do what he has promised, and his mate is always on him about what he hasn't done.

6. Passive Aggressive rarely thinks he has made a mistake and needs to apologize. When he does apologize, it is usually a maneuver to get his partner off his case. His apology does not contain a promise to change.

7. Passive Aggressive is unsure of himself; internally he feels powerless and dependent and lacks self-confidence.

8. Passive Aggressive, when confronted, defends his behavior by getting angry and turning the issue around to make his behavior someone else's responsibility. Or he uses such excuses as "I forgot" or "I'm sorry you see it that way."

9. Passive Aggressive does not see how his behavior affects others. He simply does not take others' wants and feelings into account if he wants to do something.

10. Passive Aggressive sees himself as basically a nice person, and can't understand why others often feel irritated and angry with him.

What's Your Score?

If eight or more of these items apply to one of you, there is a Passive Aggressive living in your house. If five, six, or seven characteristics apply, you or your mate may not deserve the label Passive Aggressive, but one of you has far too many discounting and inappropriate behaviors.

She Withholds Sex

To show her disapproval and to deal with her feelings of anger, sadness, and disappointment, the wife of a Passive Aggressive will frequently withhold sex. Withholding sex gives her some power in the relationship. Also, she reasons, if she has sex after her husband behaves so inappropriately, she is covertly giving him permission to continue to discount her and to repeat his bad behavior.

❧ THE PASSIVE TAKER MAN

The Passive Taker is the man who seems only vaguely aware of what goes on around him. He is not in tune with his own wants or needs or those of his mate. He is an easygoing, nice guy willing to go along with whatever his wife suggests. At the same time, he rarely makes a decision, takes responsibility, or approaches his wife sexually.

If his wife asks him whether he would like iced tea or coffee with dinner, he responds, "Whatever." If she asks if he would like to go to the movies, he says, "It's up to you." If his wife puts on a sexy new negligee, he doesn't notice.

As one woman who is married to a Passive Taker says, "I'd watch Oprah Winfrey and Donahue and all the shows, anything that had something on sex. I'd read articles in magazines and think, Is there something wrong with me? Is there something wrong with him? Then I'd discuss it with him. After one of these shows the pressure would really be on, so we'd have sex. This would satisfy me for a while, but then there would be no sex again for another four to six months. Even when we have sex, Jack's passive. He doesn't kiss me much. There isn't much foreplay. It takes all of ten to fifteen minutes. He gets an erection. We have intercourse. He's on top, then we flip over and I'm on top. He has an orgasm, then he goes to sleep. One time he said, 'Too bad that you didn't come.' But he doesn't do anything to help me."

And discussing her Passive Taker mate, a caretaker wife had this to say: "If we have sex, I do the approaching. I blow in his ear, I caress him. I play with the hairs on his chest. I work my way down. He lies there. He puts his hands over his head. I get no response except maybe a groan. This lets me know that what I'm doing is wonderful, but I get nothing back. If I keep fooling around with him, he comes, and that's that. I get nothing."

The Passive Taker Test

Now let's see if you are living with a Passive Taker, or if you are one yourself. Read over the following list and check off the items that apply to either your partner or to you.

1. Passive Taker is content doing almost anything, spends most of his free time alone, lives in his own

world, and does not have a need to interact with others.

2. Passive Taker will probably have sex if you approach him, but he rarely will take the initiative and approach you.

3. Passive Taker rarely asks his mate to do something for him. He makes few demands.

4. Passive Taker does not think in advance or plan ahead. He does not shop more than a day or two ahead for birthdays, plan for sex, call ahead for reservations, or think in terms of the future.

5. Passive Taker is not attuned to his own wants or those of his mate.

6. Passive Taker rarely gives compliments or pats on the back; nor does he recognize what others do for him.

7. Passive Taker is seldom critical of himself or his partner.

8. Passive Taker is viewed by the outside world as nice, easygoing, and content.

9. Passive Taker's spouse often accuses him of being selfish, not taking responsibility in the relationship, and just not seeming to care about anything.

10. Passive Taker is noncompetitive and prefers to let others take the lead.

What's Your Score?

If eight or more of these items apply to your mate or to you, one of you is definitely a Passive Taker. If you have checked off five, six, or seven items, one of you is still too emotionally dependent in the relationship.

He Never Approaches, She Quits Trying

At first, living with a Passive Taker is pleasant, because he is so easygoing and undemanding. But after a time the woman who is married to this type of man gets tired of making all the decisions and always being responsible for initiating sex. And at some point, three, five, or ten years into the marriage, she gives up trying to get her passive taker husband to approach her, and she stops approaching him.

&. A PASSIVE AGGRESSIVE WOMAN, A CORRECTOR MAN

Since the development of these four personality types, many people have asked me if you can be more than one type. The answer is yes and no. Although none of the categories are mutually exclusive (you can have characteristics from several different categories), most people have a heavy concentration of characteristics from one category.

The exception is the Caretaker. She may score eight points on the Caretaker test and score as high as six points on the Corrector test.

As I have explained, a woman is usually a Caretaker, a Corrector, or a Caretaker with a number of Corrector characteristics. However, a few women fall into the Passive Aggressive category, and a very small percentage fall into the Passive Taker category. Although most men qualify as Passive Aggressives or Passive Takers, some men are Correctors, and a very few are Caretakers. You will meet some of these exceptions later in this book.

❧ THE STRUGGLE FOR POWER

Power struggles are another big obstacle to making love. Many people bicker and fight regularly over who gets to make the decisions in the relationship and who has the final word. If both the husband and the wife believe strongly that it is their "right" to have the final say, they will argue "to the death" about everything. They will argue about how to spend the money, who should be able to spend more of it, who spends most of it, who does more around the house, what movies the children should be allowed to see, and how loud to play the television. In fact, the issues that couples fight about are endless. And when these arguments for control get out of hand, a couple is not going to be physically intimate—they feel hurt and angry with each other after arguing, and they do not like each other very much.

As one man confessed, "We constantly disagree about the temperature in the house. She wants the thermostat set at sixty-four degrees, winter and summer. She's always too hot and I'm always freezing. This upsets our sex life because it gets me upset. How would you like to walk around in your house and be freezing all the time?"

Another woman commented, "Since the beginning of our marriage, we have had this terrible problem—who is going to be in control. We'll be making love and what he's doing isn't satisfying me, or worse, it is turning me off. If I say, 'Please don't do that,' he gets his feelings hurt. And sometimes he gets up and leaves the bed. This is his way of controlling me. There is no room for criticism. Sometimes he stops what he's doing, but the next time he does the same thing again. I keep thinking, 'This man's intelligent. He has an incredible memory.' And yet he can't remember that this turns me off. Then I think, 'Why doesn't he listen to me?' When he doesn't do what I want him to do, I go passive. I lie in bed like a lump. So the two of us struggle for control of how our sex life is going to be."

&. THE STRUGGLE FOR ATTENTION

Many couples also struggle on a subconscious level to be the center of attention. And when these subtle power struggles are going on, sex is not likely to be part of their agenda.

For example, a wife tells her husband that she thinks she is starting to come down with a cold. The husband responds, "I think I'm getting one too." Instead of focusing on his wife's cold, this man has switched the attention from his wife to himself.

Another example is the husband who calls his wife from his office a few minutes before he is to be home for dinner. When she answers the phone, he says cheerfully, "Hi, honey, What's going on?" His cheerful "Hi, honey" routine is a maneuver to get his wife to reassure him that she's not going to be upset because he's late. Instead, this man needs to realize that his lateness is probably an inconvenience to his wife. She is the one who should be receiving the attention in the form of an explanation for his lateness as well as an apology.

There is also the wife who says to her husband, "You still don't take care of me when we make love." And her husband responds, "I think I'm doing better." Here the focus of attention has shifted from the wife feeling that her needs are not being met, to her husband feeling that he has been improving.

Then there is the wife who comes home from work and begins to tell her husband what a bad day she's had, but before she's finished with her story, her husband starts with his story about *his* bad day. This husband has subtly shifted the attention away from his wife and onto himself.

Later on that evening, as his wife starts talking about something she has read in the newspaper, he remains silent. He doesn't make any comments or ask any questions. After a few minutes she starts to become anxious, particularly if she's a Caretaker, because she feels on some level that she is not pleasing him. As her anxiety increases, she switches from what she is talking about to what he might want to talk about. She does this by asking him a question about his day. As he responds to her question, he has become the center of attention.

That evening, when he approaches her for sex, she turns him down. She's too tired. On examining why she is often too tired for sex, she admits that she doesn't feel very close to her husband. On reflection, she comes to realize that he rarely makes her feel important or the center of attention. Because of this lack of attention, she does not feel emotionally intimate.

What she doesn't understand is the dynamic of how the attention in the relationship keeps shifting away from her and onto her husband. What both she and her husband do understand, however, is that their sex life is awful.

❧ ENDLESS ROADBLOCKS TO SEX

From time to time factors other than the ones I've mentioned interfere with a couple's sex life, as the following comments attest.

No Time for Sex

"I get home from work late and start dinner. We get our son to bed. I do laundry so we have underwear. By that time it's nine o'clock. Then it's pay bills and give each other a brief rundown of what's happened during the day. Everything seems to have immediacy but sex."

A Fear of Closeness and Sex

"We have sort of a fear of getting close. When one of us is making overtures, the other person picks up on the clues and pulls away. If we spend a nice evening together, I set it up that when Alex gets back from taking the babysitter home, I'm doing something — reading, watching television, folding laundry. If, on the other hand, I put on a sexy nightgown, which signals that I'm interested in making love, it is Alex who turns on the television or starts reading."

Lack of Desire

"I have a low sex drive; I just don't desire sex. I don't even think about it!"

Infertility Problems

"One reason for not having sex is our inability to conceive a child. When we found out that we couldn't procreate, making love was sort of sad."

Not in the Habit

"I think if you get in the habit of not having a lot of sex, it's easy to maintain that pattern. That's our pattern—infrequent sex."

ꝫ HOW YOU ALONE CAN CHANGE THE DYNAMICS THAT STOP SEX AND ROMANCE

If infrequent sex or no sex has become your pattern, I think you will find the following chapters most helpful. You will undoubtedly see yourself and your partner in a number of the stories that others have shared, and you will immediately become more insightful as to why your sex life is not as good as it could be.

I found it heartening that during the year and a half that I interviewed couples for this book, a number of people telephoned a few months after meeting with me to say that they were having more sex. They also said that their relationship overall was improving.

I think the interview process started people focusing once again on their sex lives, as well as on the ways they were relating to their partners. As they started to become more introspective about what was happening between them, they began to make some changes in the way they behaved. Also, because they were thinking more about sex, they initiated it more frequently. Reading this book should have a similar effect for you.

You will also be relieved to learn that not everyone in the world is having sex two and three times a week. From my findings, most couples do not have sex twice a week. And many, many couples do not have sex once a week. At the same time, most couples are reluctant to share such information. If a man shares that he only has sex every couple of weeks, he fears that people will think less of him—even get the idea that he isn't much of a man. On the other hand, most women are reticent to share how little sex they are having because they don't want their friends to get the idea that there is something wrong with their husbands—or that there is something wrong with them because their husbands do not desire them more.

The important thing regarding sexual frequency is to think about how much sex you would ideally like to have, as well as how much sex your partner finds fulfilling, and then come to some sort of balance, with the goal of a good relationship that includes a healthy sex life.

I hope, too, that you will take comfort in finding out that other couples face some of the same struggles and disappointments in their relationship that you find yourself up against.

By identifying your personality type and that of your mate, you will instantly see how each of you is sabotaging your sex life. Most important, you will learn how you alone can change the ongoing dynamics that stop romance, sex, and intimacy.

For example, say you just learned that your husband is a Passive Aggressive. Once you come to understand why lecturing and anger only invite him to act more outrageously, and why withholding sex does not get him to change, you can start using more workable tactics, laid out in the next chapters, to get him to behave differently.

If you have recognized that you are a Corrector, and you come to understand that your critical comments about what your mate is doing wrong are causing the two of you to pull away from each other, you can stop those comments and learn to focus on the positive things that your partner brings to the relationship. Once you change your behavior, you will feel closer to him and he to you.

Besides untangling the underlying reasons why sex has become too infrequent, you will find out how you can immediately renew your sex life. In fact, you will learn over 100 effective techniques that you can use by yourself to change the dynamics in your marriage.

As changes start to occur—and they will, if you follow but a few of the suggestions in this book—you and your mate will start having a stronger, healthier, more loving relationship. And you will reexperience the emotional and physical intimacy that sex brings to marriage.

CHAPTER TWO

THE MAIN REASON FOR INFREQUENT SEX—
THE PASSIVE AGGRESSIVE MAN

In this chapter you will meet Tom. Tom is a classic Passive Aggressive. He does what he wants to do, when he wants to do it, both in and out of the bedroom. As a result of Tom's behavior, his wife, Anne, frequently feels frustrated and angry with him. To show her disapproval of his actions, as well as to take care of her own feelings of hurt and frustration, Anne frequently refuses to have sex with Tom.

❧ THE MAN WHO DID AS HE DAMN WELL PLEASED

Anne and Tom are in their mid-thirties. They have been married for twelve years. Before marriage they lived together for about a year and a half. They have three children, 11, 9, and 8.

Anne's Story

We have sex about every three weeks, although we may not have sex for six weeks at a time. I think it's because I'm always angry at Tom. I have an internal growl at all times. You might say my feelings for Tom are the opposite of friendly.

Our sex life seems to revolve around Tom's performance rather than enjoying each other. He is always focused on his erection. Usually we'll be watching T.V. after the kids are in bed. He'll reach down and grab me in the crotch, kiss me on the neck and say, "Let's do it." Boy does that get me! I feel like he's a dirty little boy when he does that.

I can't count the number of times I've told him not to approach me that way. It's a turn-off. I'm looking for someone to hold me and cuddle me and to say, "It's nice to have you to come home to."

When I tell Tom I hate his approach, he comes back with, "It's natural for a man to react that way. Why can't you lighten up?" That makes me angry, too, because he's implying that there is something wrong with me because I don't like his approach.

Usually one of two things will happen after Tom comes on to me. I'll tell him no sex, and that's that. Or we'll go into the bedroom and I'll try to push down my feelings about the way he has approached me.

He'll usually kiss my breasts and then he wants to have oral sex on me. There are only two erotic zones, as far as he's concerned—my breasts and my vagina.

BORING! There is no conversation about sex unless it's dirty. I think sex should be an expression of our caring. It should be warm and fun, but it's not.

Tom doesn't want me to have oral sex on him, so generally I'm pretty passive. To me it feels like he's the director. It seems that he is more interested in making me have a climax than in relaxing and enjoying our coming together. At some point I'll maneuver around or he turns around and we have intercourse. He comes, but usually I don't. Sometimes he masturbates me. Often I'm content to have the whole thing over with.

Tom's solution is always that we should have sex more often. He says he could be more romantic if he weren't so horny and always thinking about getting a little. He approaches me almost every day. He doesn't quit trying.

What I find stimulating is a good conversation. I have that with my friends, but not with Tom. If we have a conversation, it's about finances, the kids, the house, the car, problems. He seems to have little interest in my life and what is important to me. He only seems interested in me sexually. It's "I'm horny. You should take care of me."

If we did more in common—cooking together, walking in the woods—I think we'd get along a lot better and I wouldn't be so angry. If he'd spend more time alone with me, I'd find him attractive.

It seems to me that Tom only does what he needs to do to get by in life. This annoys me. He doesn't do his paperwork. He's forever late on his sales tax. We get threatening letters from the Internal Revenue Service. He has a real contempt for authority. It's almost as if he's saying, "Knock the chip off my shoulder."

He drives whatever speed he chooses. He says there shouldn't be speed limits. People know when they're going too fast.

Our town has a leash law. He says that's a stupid law. Dogs shouldn't be put on a chain. So he lets our dog run.

I don't tell him any more about the things that I don't like because he has a real hairpin trigger. He goes beyond anger to rage. The veins stick out on his neck, he grits his teeth, he clenches his fist.

I'm not the only person he unleashes his anger on. He's real big at calling the children names when he's angry. It's "You stupid little jerk" or "You damn kids."

If something of his is missing, he immediately blames it on the children. If he later discovers that they didn't take the missing item, he will never apologize. Instead he says, "Well, they are usually the ones who take my things."

He just doesn't take responsibility for his own actions. It's always someone else's fault! It's the government's, it's the kid's, it's the car's. Quite often it's my fault. If he apologizes, he also defends. He says, "I'm sorry that I got so angry, but YOU could make anyone angry."

He doesn't pick up his clothes. We've discussed it a million times. Eventually I pick them up, but I resent it.

How much sex we have is a good barometer of what's happening in our everyday life. I will approach him if things are going okay, if he is being nice. Sometimes I find myself approaching Tom after he's gone to sleep. Maybe that's when I like him the best.

When I was a kid, my father never expressed his love. If I said, "I love you," he would say "Thank you." When my dad went to sleep, I used to carefully lift his arm and wrap it around me. I put my head on his shoulder and I'd go to sleep next to him. I remember how he smelled. How warm and secure I felt snuggled up against him. I felt like he loved me when I was that close to him.

One way that Tom expresses his love for me—he draws pictures on the envelopes of greeting cards he gives me, little wonderful things. It touches my heart. Sometimes he makes me a cup of coffee and leaves it on the counter. He protects me from the kids if I'm sick. If I have a headache and lie down, he closes the bedroom door. He intercepts the kids before they get to me. There are a lot of times when he's a nice guy.

He can be very sensitive and tender to his children, and he's as loyal as an old dog. He makes friends easily, and he enjoys doing things for other people. He's intelligent and handsome. I love him. It's just that I don't like how he acts sometimes. I resent that Tom always does what he damn well pleases."

Showing Disapproval by Withholding Sex

Although Tom has a number of wonderful characteristics and Anne readily admits that she loves him, it's easy to see why she denies him sex. His outrageous behavior drives her away.

When one partner does whatever he pleases, it sets in motion the process whereby his mate attempts to show her disapproval by withholding sex. This is the number-one reason why couples do not have sex more frequently.

And now a look at the Passive Aggressive in depth.

ૐ THE PASSIVE AGGRESSIVE

The Passive Aggressive focuses mainly on himself. He operates from a position that he counts more than you count, and as a result, he does pretty much as he pleases. If he wants to be a nice guy, he's a nice guy. If he wants to act like the only person in the world who counts, he acts like he's the only person in the world who counts.

One day a Passive Aggressive will promise to do something for you and the next day he will change his mind. Frequently, however, he does not tell you he has changed his mind. As a result, you keep waiting for him to do what he has promised.

A Passive Aggressive will often make you wait because he gets involved with something else. He doesn't consciously think, "I'll keep her waiting," but he does keep you waiting, because what he wants to do takes priority.

People are sometimes confused by the term Passive Aggressive, and they wonder how someone can be both passive and aggressive simultaneously. Here's how it works.

The Passive Aggressive tells you he'll be home by six and he doesn't come home until six-thirty. His behavior is aggressive because he has discounted you. At the same time, he hasn't struck you physically, or called you names, or thrown a temper tantrum, behaviors that we typically think of as aggressive. His aggression has been expressed passively.

Here's another scenario. Passive Aggressive calls and tells you to hurry and get ready for a night out; he has just gotten baseball tickets. You say okay and hurry to get ready. In the meantime Passive Aggressive decides that he's really too tired to go to the game, but he doesn't call and tell you he has changed his mind.

Making a unilateral decision that the two of you are not going to the game—after the two of you have agreed to go—

is aggressive behavior. But the aggressive behavior has been expressed passively.

A Nasty Temper

In addition to expressing aggression passively, many Passive Aggressives have very nasty tempers. Remember that it is standard operating procedure for the Passive Aggressive to do what he pleases. So if you confront him about his behavior, he's likely to get angry, turn things around, and confront you on something he doesn't like about your behavior.

Recall Anne's repeated request that Tom be more romantic, instead of grabbing her in the crotch and saying "Let's do it." Tom's excuse was that he could be more romantic if he "weren't so horny and wasn't always thinking about getting a little." This excuse shifts responsibility and implies that Anne is to blame for his unromantic approach.

When you confront a Passive Aggressive, his usual response is to defend and become angry. If you get angry, he gets more angry. As a result, you will usually back down. Thus, once again, Passive Aggressive gets his way. His behavior has been reinforced; he counts more than anyone else.

A Sensitive Person

What is so confusing about a Passive Aggressive is that he is often a caring and sensitive person. In fact, he will go out of his way to do nice things for you. The catch is—he takes care of you only when it's convenient for him. Or he takes

care of you in the way that he wants, rather than consider-
ing how you may want him to take care of you.

Perhaps this is why almost every Passive Aggressive
gets in trouble with his wife over gift giving. He thinks
about what he wants to buy rather than what his wife
might like.

One man I saw in therapy, who was clearly a "10" on
the passive aggressive test, decided to surprise his wife and
whisk her away to New York for her 35th birthday. His plan
was to leave on Friday morning and return Sunday evening. In order to pull things off, he had to call his wife's
boss and make arrangements with her office. He got airline
tickets, hotel reservations, and tickets for several plays. He
sneaked clothes from the closet and packed her bags. On
Friday, instead of driving her to work, he planned to take
her to New York. He made all these plans with great care
and anticipation.

When this man told his therapy group what he was up
to, we predicted disaster. Why? *Because his wife hated to
be surprised.* Moreover, he was discounting the kind of
birthday celebration his wife would choose in favor of the
kind of birthday he wanted to give her.

I still remember one woman in the group saying, "If my
husband did that to me I'd be furious. At least tell her what
you have in mind, so that if she's absolutely against it, the
two of you can make other plans." Unfortunately, our arguments and advice went unheeded, and off to New York
they went.

Predictably, his wife was angry. Because her husband
had made such elaborate plans, however, she hid her ir-
ritation and disappointment and tried to make the best of

it. But her birthday weekend was not what she had hoped for. Furthermore, the clothes he had packed, which had been hung in the hall closet, were ones that had been scheduled to be given away.

There she was in New York, where she didn't want to be, on her birthday, in clothes she had already decided to give away, struggling to have a grand time.

One passive aggressive fellow gave his wife a VCR for her birthday. The only problem—she never watches television. As this woman told the story, she half laughed and said, "He even helped me unwrap the damn thing." She was able to laugh when she told the story, but I'm sure that on her birthday she was very disappointed.

Another Passive Aggressive gave his wife a beautiful wool sweater for her birthday. The problem: she is highly allergic to wool. When she pointed out that the sweater was wool, he responded indignantly, "But Betty, it's your color."

Never an Apology

Another frustrating trait of the Passive Aggressive is that he rarely takes responsibility for his mistakes, nor does he apologize. Remember Tom's typical response when he finds out that the children actually did not take a missing item? He would excuse his inappropriate behavior entirely by saying, "Well, they are always taking my things."

The reason a Passive Aggressive doesn't apologize is that he has trouble seeing that he has made a mistake. If by chance you do get an apology, it's likely to be just a maneuver to get you off his case. Typical apologies are "I'm sorry you feel that way" and "I'm sorry you see it that way."

Note that these apologies put the responsibility back on you and imply that you are misinterpreting the situation and making a big deal out of nothing.

The other discouraging thing about a Passive Aggressive's apology is that it does not contain a promise to change. The reason is that Passive Aggressive simply does not see that he has erred. That's why, the next day or the next week, he'll repeat the same behavior.

You, Too, Will Become Aggressive

In dealing with a Passive Aggressive, you often wind up feeling aggressive yourself. Or you turn the aggression inward and feel depressed.

He's late, and you get angry. He mows over your flowers, and you get depressed. He leaves his dirty dishes all over the place, and you feel irritated. In addition, you must struggle with the issue of whether you'll clean up the mess yourself or wait for him to clean it up.

A particularly infuriating dynamic when dealing with a Passive Aggressive is that he feels innocent of any wrongdoing and doesn't understand why his behavior causes such a negative response in you. He is not leaving the dishes around as a way to punish you. He does not break his promise because he is trying to get back at you. He does not hate you. He is simply doing what he wants. In doing what he wants, however, he discounts you. Because you are continually being discounted, you experience many negative feelings that disrupt your sex life.

Sex with a Passive Aggressive

Sexually a Passive Aggressive can be the best of lovers or the worst of lovers. He may withhold sex or demand sex. But having sex is always on his terms—when you have it and how you have it. If he thinks it is important to bring you to orgasm, he will insist on doing so, even if you have told him that you would like him to stop stimulating you. If he feels like pinching your breast, he'll do it even if you've told him repeatedly that this behavior is a turn-off. In the morning Passive Aggressive may call you names and threaten a divorce. Yet that very night he'll act like nothing has happened and he'll expect sex. If you turn him down because of his earlier behavior, he'll become indignant and act as though there is something wrong with you. How he acts in regard to sex is just like how he acts about everything else. He does what he pleases.

A woman who is married to a Passive Aggressive will often not initiate sex or respond to her husband's overtures. It's not that she has a problem and dislikes sex; rather, she feels as though she cannot be intimate when his behavior repeatedly implies that she doesn't count. Unfortunately, withholding sex does not get a Passive Aggressive to look at his behavior and change. In fact, it often has the opposite effect. He uses his wife's withholding as a way to justify and excuse even more of his discounting behavior.

&. HOW TO LIVE WITH A PASSIVE AGGRESSIVE WITHOUT WITHHOLDING SEX

Now, how do you deal with a Passive Aggressive without falling into negative behavior yourself? How do you avoid getting angry or becoming depressed? How do you cope without refusing to approach your partner sexually or turning him down when he approaches you?

The first step is to keep remembering that a Passive Aggressive thinks differently from you. His discounting behavior is a way to take care of himself. It is not a way to be mean to you. Simply understanding this should help you feel less hostile toward some of his actions, at least some of the time.

The second important step in dealing with a Passive Aggressive is to decide beforehand how you will handle some of those behaviors of his that drive you crazy. For example, how will you deal with him when he breezes in at 7 p.m. when he has repeatedly agreed to be home by 6:30?

You might decide to eat dinner alone on those nights, and to be pleasant when he arrives, but not reheat or serve his dinner. The problem with this decision, of course, is that you lose out on spending time with him. If you value spending time with him, that's painful. If you have children, they lose out on having dinner with their father.

Nevertheless, if he consistently comes in late, having a plan to put in motion will help you feel more in control and certainly less frustrated.

Remember, few people make love when they are angry at their mate. So anything you can do to help yourself feel less angry is going to have a positive impact on your sex life.

Send Him a Note

Here's another example of how to deal with a Passive Aggressive. Let's suppose that Passive Aggressive has agreed to put out the trash on Tuesdays and Fridays. True to his nature, he "forgets" and does it only half the time.

Your plan might be that when he doesn't put out the trash, you will put it out and only allow yourself to feel mildly irritated. Or you can decide that no matter how long it sits, or how much it smells, you're never going to put the trash out—because in retrospect, you see that that's how you became the one responsible for paying bills, cutting the grass, hanging the wallpaper, and doing the taxes.

Regardless of what decision you make about the trash, however, you will only allow yourself to become mildly annoyed. You will not yell or lecture about how irresponsible he is or how you can't count on him for anything.

To dissipate some of your negative feelings, as well as make your point that he hasn't kept his agreement, you might put a note on the counter that reads, "I put out the trash. Please remember next time." A few hundred notes will probably do the trick. No joking. A gentle reminder with little anger really does get a Passive Aggressive to change.

Remember the way Tom approached Anne for sex? He would grab her in the crotch and say, "Let's do it." What Anne might do is take Tom's hand and say somewhat flirtatiously, "Hold on, Tom, let's sit and smooch a little first, and then we can do it." Again, after a few hundred times, Tom will get the message and Anne will not feel so helpless. Remember, too, that Tom hasn't gotten the message by Anne's refusing sex—so another tactic is certainly in order.

Here are a few other techniques you can use when dealing with your Passive Aggressive.

Stick with the Issue

One important skill is the ability to stick with the issue when you confront Passive Aggressive.

Suppose, for example, that Anne confronts Tom on leaving his messy clothes around. And he responds, "Well, the cleaning lady is coming tomorrow."

Anne needs to be careful not to focus on the cleaning lady. Instead she might say, "The cleaning lady is not the issue. The issue is that you left your clothes in the den."

Chances are Tom will try again to redefine the issue. This time he might try to bring Anne directly into the problem by saying something provocative, such as, "Since when have you gotten so picky about how this place looks?"

Again, Anne needs to stick with the original issue of Tom's clothes, saying something like, "Tom, come on, pick up your clothes." Being forced to stick with the issue will prevent a Passive Aggressive from focusing on something else and may get him at least to look at his behavior—the first step towards change.

If nothing seems to get him to pick up his clothes, you will have to decide if you are willing to pick them up or whether you can tolerate his clothes lying around.

Remember—complaining, pouting, or having a temper tantrum about his clothes will not get him to change. These tactics will only invite him to focus on your "unreasonableness" instead of his inappropriate behavior.

Don't Rehash Old Offenses

Another important skill—make your confrontation and then stop. Do not go on and on. This is particularly hard because a Passive Aggressive tends to repeat his annoying behaviors. And you already have a long ledger of past insults stored up. So when Passive Aggressive hasn't done what he promised to do for the 500th time, it's easy to get on a roll and replay all the old insults and call forth all the old feelings that go with these offenses.

When you're tempted to rehash the injustices and slights of the past, use this technique. Think of life as a kind of film strip that keeps moving along. As the film rolls, the scenes change and so do your feelings. As life moves along, keep updating your feelings; don't get stuck too long on one of the previous frames.

So often I'll see a couple for marriage counseling who are furious with each other about something that happened days before. In the meantime, however, they've gone to the movies, laughed with friends at a party, and had several nice evenings together.

When you dwell too much on a disappointment or argument that has occurred several days before, say to yourself, "Move on, the film is rolling. Move on, the film is rolling." And then do not allow yourself to go back and rehash the argument in your head.

Although your mate has disappointed you at six, you can still decide to go for a walk with him at seven, laugh with him at eight, and respond to his approach for sex at nine.

Refusing Sex Will Not Change a Passive Aggressive

Remember, repeatedly refusing sex will not get a Passive Aggressive to change. It will shut off the opportunity for closeness and intimacy, as well as the good feelings that couples experience toward each other after they have sex. So don't use this tactic. In the long run, it will only cause more dissatisfaction with the relationship.

CHAPTER THREE

ANOTHER REASON FOR INFREQUENT SEX— THE CORRECTOR WOMAN

"It's hard to make love to someone who is always correcting you, lecturing you, analyzing you, and pointing out your flaws," says Ralph.

"Well" says Janette, "It's equally hard to make love to someone who continually does the dumbest, stupidest, hare-brained things. . . ."

If you're the woman who is forever criticizing and focusing on your partner's flaws, it won't be long before you lose sight of his good qualities. If, on the other hand, you're the husband who is always being called on the carpet, you're certainly not going to be feeling very good about yourself. Nor is it likely that you will feel very affectionate toward your wife.

When one partner corrects, criticizes, and continually focuses on her mate's flaws, it creates the process whereby the partner who is being criticized retreats—physically and emotionally. This is the second most common reason couples do not have sex more frequently.

ℯ THE WOMAN WHO TOOK OFFENSE AT THE HORSERADISH

In this interview you hear about Kay, who can frequently be heard correcting Mike, her husband. In addition, you will see how Mike's provocative behavior has invited Kay to become a Corrector.

Kay and Mike are in their late thirties and have three children.

Mike's Story

We make love once, maybe twice, a month. This does not satisfy me, nor my wife, Kay. When we have sex, it's good in terms of the physical pleasures. She always reaches orgasm. But there is often something in the way of our having sex. One of us is unhappy about some issue. I know my dissatisfaction with Kay is reflected in my lack of sexual interest. It's hard to make love to her when she's always criticizing me.

Kay doesn't feel taken care of in our marriage. She doesn't think I pay enough attention to her. According to her, I don't initiate hugs or physical contact. I don't suggest things for us to do together. I don't make enough money. I'm not advancing as rapidly as I should. I don't do enough as a father. When I look back, I think I might have done more with the children when they were babies, but my personal assessment is that I am very involved in their activities now.

One of the things Kay complains about is that I
don't do enough around the house. I think she's right.
So I agreed to do all the vacuuming. But then she didn't
like the way I vacuumed. I didn't use the nozzle to
vacuum the extreme edges around the baseboard. When
I see dirt accumulating, I will put on the nozzle and do
it, but I am not going to do it every time.

Kay is a terrible back-seat driver. I'm always in the
wrong lane. She picks, picks, picks. Nothing I do is
right. She's not satisfied with the way I dress. She thinks
I'm stodgy. She tells me I dress too conservatively for
business. She can be very critical about my table manners. I think I have good manners. Recently she gave
me a column to read from Miss Manners about people
who reach over and take food off someone else's plate.
I said, "Kay, I don't do that!"

I like horseradish on a lot of things. Once at dinner
I excused myself to get the horseradish. She said that
if the cook hadn't provided a certain condiment, it was
terribly impolite to use it. I agree—if we're at someone
else's house. I would never ask the hostess to bring me
a condiment that wasn't on the table. But in my own
home I think I should be able to use what I want.

I remember one time we were coming home from
vacation and Kay was terribly ill. She told me to wake
her when we got to Baton Rouge. I still felt fresh and
wide-awake when we got there so I let her sleep. When
she woke up, she blasted me because I hadn't done
what she told me to do. I felt especially bad because I
thought I was being considerate.

I had a company car that I got a chance to buy. It
was two years old; the mileage was low. She didn't like
the car. We debated back and forth. She finally agreed
that we should buy it. Even though the car runs great
and we have had no problems with it, in her eyes there
is nothing right with it. She is constantly noticing things
that are wrong.

Through the years I have become resentful and I have stopped feeling affectionate toward her. At this point the desire to hug her, or kiss her, or be close to her, or even have a nice conversation with her has dissipated. It has gotten to the point where I don't want to be close sexually or any other way.

I know there are always two sides to a story. In the early years we had a lot of fun. I loved her a lot. She is a good person. She is a great mother. She takes good care of the kids. She goes to all their school conferences. She takes them to all their doctor and dental appointments. She does the majority of the housework. She makes all of our social arrangements. She also has a job. She does a lot!

I also developed a drinking problem over the years, and this has had an impact on my life with Kay. I drank socially until about six years ago when I found myself looking forward to opportunities to drink. I'd get home in the evening and have two or three drinks before dinner. I used to race to see how many drinks I could gulp down before Kay could get dinner on the table.

I'd eat dinner, and afterwards, with the food and alcohol, I'd be lethargic. I'd be slow to do things around the house. I'd promise to do something and then I wouldn't complete it. Kay would be angry, which I understand. When I'd do a job I'd spend fifty percent more time on it than I should have just to make it so grand that she couldn't find anything wrong with it. I always saw myself as a victim. I felt like a child—she was my parent. I was the jerk who couldn't do anything right.

I went to AA at Kay's urging and now I have stopped drinking. Unfortunately, things have only gotten worse between us. I've become interested in taking a more active role in the family. As long as I was drinking, I was willing to go with the flow.

Kay is not used to having me involved in making the decisions. She is not prepared to give up running the family. She also will not get involved with Al-Anon.

She can't see that my drinking affected her behavior. She thinks our kids have been affected, and she is more than happy to point that out to me.

The odd part of it all is that she says she wants to have someone who makes decisions and takes control. But when I take control, such as when I pushed her to buy the company car, she doesn't like it.

We agree that we need to make some investments. I took some classes on money management. I came home with a lot of ideas about what we should do. She vetoed every one of them. Then she criticizes me about not making enough money.

It's hard to make love to someone who is always on you about something, even if the criticism is valid some of the time.

🍃 Even the Desire to Hug Her Has Disappeared

It's clear that the reason Mike is not very attracted to Kay is that she is so critical of him. Even though many of Kay's criticisms are valid, they still sting. They still cause resentment to build. In fact, each time Kay makes a critical comment, Mike feels a little more distant, to the point where "the desire to hug her, or kiss her, or be close to her . . . has dissipated."

When Mike was drinking, he was able to tune out some of Kay's critical remarks. I suspect, too, that he was more willing to accept her criticism because he knew his behavior was out of line.

When Mike got into Alcoholics Anonymous and changed some of his behaviors, the dynamics in the relationship also changed. No longer did Mike see himself as the bad guy deserving constant criticism. Nor did he see Kay as doing everything right. As Mike observes, "As long as I was drinking, I was willing to go with the flow. Kay is not used to having me involved in making the decisions. She is not prepared to give up running the family."

Even though it was Kay who suggested AA, she has been unwilling to participate in Mike's treatment. As a result, she has not been able to see that she, too, has developed some unhealthy behaviors through the years, such as taking over the majority of responsibilities in the family, feeling continually resentful, and focusing too much on her husband's flaws.

In the beginning of this marriage, Kay was undoubtedly the Caretaker. By Mike's own admission, Kay took care of everything. What happens to many Caretakers, however, and it certainly seems to have happened to Kay, is that, after years of taking care of others, they get emotionally tired. No longer can they do it all—they're older, and their responsibilities have usually increased. Along the way, most Caretakers also start to feel resentful, and they think, "Hey, when do I get taken care of around here?"

As the Caretaker struggles to shift some of the responsibilities that she once so willingly accepted, she finds herself irritated that her husband and children do not see what needs to be done. In addition, she has been doing things her way for so many years that she expects her mate to do things exactly as she would. When her husband doesn't do it the way she thinks it should be done, she turns critical. Many women start out as Caretakers and wind up as Correctors.

In Kay's defense, Mike's behavior certainly provided her with plenty to correct—his failure to keep promises, his drinking, his lethargy, his procrastination, and even his rebellion.

At the same time, Kay became too critical of too many things (for example, her objection to her husband's excusing himself from the dinner table to get the horseradish).

&. "WE DON'T MAKE LOVE MORE BECAUSE OF THE HOSTILITY I FEEL"

In this next interview you will hear about Corrector Toni and how her constant complaining has become a sexual turnoff to her husband George. Toni and George, who have been married for nine years, make love "once every two to three months." Both are thirty-two years old. They have three children, ages 6, 4, and 2.

George's Story

The reason we do not make love more is because of the pressure of my job and the hostility I feel toward Toni.

I work about sixty hours a week and I'm tired in the evenings. On the weekends we have a lot of friction because Toni gives me helpful hints about things that need to get done.

The other night we were standing outside talking and she says, "That space under the deck looks terrible. Why can't you clean that up and sow some grass seed under there? Also we should think about putting in a patio." Then she says, "But you're too busy with work. Your work always comes first." Instead of dealing with one issue and solving that, everything becomes an opportunity for her to complain.

Whatever time there is, Toni says I give it to the children. She feels there is never anything left for her. I guess that's somewhat true. I really don't give her enough time. But when she criticizes me, I don't want to spend time with her. It's like a self-fulfilling prophecy.

Over the years I have felt that we have less and less to talk about. She's not interested in my work because she resents it. And work is such a big part of my life because of its time requirements. I don't have a lot of other things to share with her. She's also unwilling to socialize with my friends from the office because they represent work to her. I wish that she would want to get to know my friends for me.

Sex. It's not a high priority with me, and Toni is pretty shy about sex. Actually we're both kind of shy. Neither of us talks about it. If we do talk about sex, it is in the context of her criticizing me for not being more sexually active. To me, sex is an expression of how good you feel about someone. And right now I don't feel very good about her.

She is not the woman I married. When I look at her, I see a woman who is constantly critical of me. I don't see a partner. I don't love her like I used to. I want to love her again. Maybe if I put more effort into showing her that I cared about her, that I noticed her, she would have more self-esteem.

When we were first married, she had a career and a much higher opinion of herself. She got gratification from something other than me. Now she's just with the kids. She has little interaction with adults. I think she's too dependent on me for her self-esteem, and I don't take care of that part of her. I don't give her the positive reinforcement she needs. I think this causes her to be critical. And then I give her less.

There were a couple of times when she approached me for sex and for one reason or another it wasn't right for me and I turned her down. Being sensitive, she hasn't approached me again. And since I haven't been very interested, we don't have much sex. When we have sex, it's okay. I think there is a lack of passion on her part. She's not willing to try different positions, though I'm as guilty as she is on that one.

When I feel good about us, when we're getting along, being loving to each other, I approach her. I have never approached her out of a purely physical need. I only approach her when I feel good about us emotionally. This is the reason I would never play around on the side. I find it difficult to have sex unless I feel emotionally comfortable.

And now, a look at the Corrector personality in depth.

❧ THE CORRECTOR

A Corrector is a person whose main focus in life seems to be finding the flaw and pointing it out. Correctors, as we have seen, think that there is a right way to do everything— cut the grass, put forks in the dishwasher, and make love. And they are more than happy to enlighten others.

Correctors expect perfection of themselves as well as everyone else. Internally they are driven by messages to work hard, to get the job done, and to be perfect. Of the four personality types, it is the Corrector who is most demanding of herself. If a Corrector does ten things right and one thing wrong, it is the thing that she has done wrong that she centers on. She beats herself up with a lot of "shoulds" and "oughts": "I should do this" and "I ought to do that."

A Corrector is a woman who wants to be in charge. However, instead of immediately jumping in and doing the job herself, as a Caretaker would, a Corrector is more likely to look over the situation and tell others what to do. Often she can be seen wagging her index finger as she does her directing. A wagging index finger is usually a direct giveaway that you are dealing with a Corrector.

Most Correctors look upon their correcting as helpful and do not realize that it causes others to pull away. And while they might feel good each time they make a helpful comment, the person to whom the comment is directed feels resentful.

One Corrector woman whom I was working with in therapy confessed that she didn't know what to talk about or what to say to people if she wasn't offering helpful hints during the conversation. Yet she could clearly see that what she termed "helpful suggestions" caused people to react negatively and pull away from her.

On the Way to the Guillotine

Perhaps better than any other example, the following joke shows just how far a Corrector will go—despite the consequences. Once upon a time there were three women who had been condemned to the guillotine.

When it was time for the executions to begin, the first woman dutifully put her head on the block. The executioner hit the trip lever and the blade came roaring down. About two inches before the blade made contact with the condemned woman's neck, the mechanism jammed. As fate seemed to have interceded, the executioner allowed the woman to go free.

The second prisoner approached the guillotine and placed her neck on the block. As before, the blade jammed, and the woman was set free.

The third prisoner approached and put her neck on the block. But before the executioner could trip the lever, the woman stretched her head around, and looking up at the mechanism of the guillotine she said, "Ah-ha . . . I see the problem."

The Sex Life of a Corrector

Because Correctors often think there is only one way to do things, and because they are ruled by a lot of "shoulds" and "oughts," they are usually quite rigid. This rigidity frequently interferes with sex. They think that there is a time and a place for sex. And they have difficulty being playful and trying a new location or a new position, because this means giving up their notion of how sex should happen.

What interferes the most with sex, however, is that because a Corrector is so focused on the flaws of her mate, she frequently loses sight of his good qualities. And if you cannot see someone's good qualities, you are simply not going to feel romantic or sexually interested.

If you're married to a Corrector, it's difficult to feel loving and sexually turned-on when you've been told two hours before that you made a mess of trimming the bushes and asked, "Why can't you ever do anything right?"

ॐ IF YOU ARE A CORRECTOR

If you recognize that you are a Corrector and you are having less physical intimacy than you would like, make a decision to change. Start by deciding to write down all the sarcastic and critical comments you hear yourself making. Although writing these remarks down will be a nuisance and somewhat painful to look at, it is better to accept this pain than the pain that generally accompanies living in a sexless marriage. Moreover, the pain of recognizing how critical you are will eventually disappear as you become less critical. Don't forget to include in your list the more subtle critical comments, such as,

"When was the last time you polished those shoes?"

"Do you realize that's the second day you've worn that shirt?"

"Are you going to pass the salad, or are you going to keep it all for yourself?"

"Why do you insist on taking this busy highway to your mother's house?"

Once you become aware of how often you are critical, you have taken the first step toward change.

The Next Step

Each time you hear yourself make a critical comment to your mate, tell yourself two things you find attractive about him. This exercise will help you change your frame of reference from noticing the negative to noticing the positive.

Make a pact that you will make no more than seven critical comments a week, and then stick to this agreement.

Also, *do* stop expecting perfection of yourself. One of the first things I do in therapy when I'm working with a Corrector is to have her make a list of 100 things she likes about herself. Then I have her read over this list each day. Remember, Correctors are hard workers. They can be counted on. And they get the job done. All they need to change is their focus from the negative to the positive. In light of this, you may also find the following story helpful.

On Weeding a Garden

A woman goes to weed her vegetable garden. She starts by pulling the biggest and most obvious weeds. Then she goes after the smaller ones. As she stands to survey her work, she spies more weeds. So again she weeds.

An hour more of weeding, and once again she stands to look over what she has accomplished. There, under the foliage of the eggplants, she notices still more weeds. But this time, instead of bending down to pull the hidden weeds, she says, "It's good enough."*

When you find yourself wanting to point out one more spot that your husband missed as he was cleaning the kitchen counter, say to yourself instead, "It's good enough. It's good enough."

---

* From *Water Bears No Scars* by David K. Reynolds. Copyright © 1987 by David K. Reynolds. Reprinted by permission of William Morrow & Co.

❧ IF YOUR MATE IS A CORRECTOR

If you find from reading this book that your mate is a Corrector, use this approach. Write down for a period of two weeks each of the critical comments your partner directs at you, such as "Why can't you ever put your dishes in the dishwasher?" and "What did you do to the coffee this morning? It tasted terrible!" Don't be surprised if, in the beginning, you count thirty or forty critical comments per day.

Once you have your list, review it carefully and see how your behavior may be inviting such remarks. After all, if you keep leaving your dirty dishes around, you are subconsciously asking to be criticized.

Once you change those behaviors of yours that are provocative, your wife's criticisms should lessen.

Now you're ready for step two. In this phase you should inform your wife that every time you hear her being critical, you are going to point it out. You might say kindly, "You're being critical." She will not be pleased with this confrontation, but she must start hearing herself and what she is doing to you—and to your love for her.

Keep in mind, too, that no one learns to play tennis well in a few weeks. So be patient and give her time to change.

As she changes, let her know that you see her changing. Tell her that you are aware that she is not making negative comments.

Once your partner becomes less critical, chances are good that you will feel more loving toward her and she will feel the same toward you. And you will have successfully changed the dynamics of the marriage.

Having sex, then, will only be a few compliments, hugs, and kisses away.

CHAPTER FOUR

THE CARETAKER WOMAN

When a woman does too much both physically and emotionally in a relationship, it follows that the man does too little. Over time this imbalance causes major problems. The wife feels burdened and taken advantage of; the husband feels smothered and somewhat guilty and frequently pulls away.

In the following interview you will see how this dynamic is played out. Marsha is a classic Caretaker, the woman who does too much in the relationship. Ken is a Passive Aggressive, the man who does what he darn well pleases.

&. THE EIGHT-YEAR DROUGHT

Marsha and Ken have been married for 26 years and are in their late forties. They have four children, two of whom are still living at home. For the past eight years, they have had almost no sex.

Marsha's Story

We don't make love because I'm alienated from Ken. I guess making love is not even an appropriate word in our case. When we did it, it was more like mating time.

All the care giving and interest in the relationship, all the reaching out and holding hands, all the pats on the shoulder, all the comforting moves, being playful—it was all up to me.

If I'd give Ken a hug, he'd stand there and take it, but he wouldn't give back. That went on for about the first ten to twelve years of our marriage. Over time my interest waned.

In the early years Ken also traveled a great deal on business. He'd go out of town on Sunday or Monday and come back Friday night. He never called during the week to touch base.

When he came home on weekends, he'd get together with his best friend on Friday night or for half a day on Saturday. Sometimes we'd go out on Friday or Saturday night with another couple. By Sunday he'd be thinking about leaving town again. Would you believe I'd even pack his suitcase?

There was so little time for us. If we did have sex, it was because the biological urge was so strong. It was just hormones leaping around.

I took care of the children and all the household stuff. If Ken got a big order at work, I'd send flowers or balloons. I did all the Christmas shopping and packaging. This was a big deal because all the gifts had to be mailed. We have lived in five different states during the course of our marriage.

When our first child was born, my labor was induced so I could have the baby on the weekend when Ken was in town, if you can believe that! Then he left on Monday.

About a year and a half later we moved to another state and I had another child. Now he didn't travel so much, but by that time I was pretty disenchanted with Ken. Even biologically I wasn't as turned on. I was tired. It was a new city. I had to go through making new friends again. Maybe at that time we had sex a few times a month.

When Ken and I had sex, it was satisfying as far as the physical aspects. But there was no communication or 'sweet nothings' in the marriage. There was never the aura of love or romance. So my desire for sex kind of died.

After a while I started avoiding sex by going to bed late. Or I'd go to bed earlier than Ken and fall asleep. I guess I thought avoiding sex would get Ken to notice me. But it didn't.

One night about eight years ago Ken approached me for sex and I said angrily, 'Don't touch me.' I tried to explain to Ken that I didn't want him to touch me because I needed more than just sex. I needed for him to talk to me and hug me and be interested in me outside the bedroom. After that night I occasionally made advances and he would respond. But he never made any overtures to me again.

Two or three years later I started to think that maybe he was involved with someone else. I would smell perfume on his shirts when I was doing the laundry. Sometimes I'd go to his car and see if I could smell that same perfume I was always smelling.

I started noticing what he wore on Wednesday because that was the day his office closed early. One day he came home with lipstick on his shirt, so I knew my suspicions were well founded. But I didn't say anything at the time because I thought he would deny it. I wanted to have all my ducks in a row.

I began going through his drawers. I looked through his daily diary. I found a key tucked in the diary and a folded motel receipt. I then started examining the charge card receipts and found regular charges at one particular motel.

I called a locksmith and told him that I had acquired some belongings from a deceased person and had several keys. I described the key and he said, "Oh, that's a special type of security key, usually a locker or motel key." Since I already had the charge card information, I knew.

On a Wednesday I drove into the motel parking lot and waited for his car. As I was sitting there waiting, here he comes out of the motel with his friend. She was walking behind him. I think Ken saw me because he put his head down. I was panic-stricken. I drove out of the parking lot as fast as I could.

That afternoon Ken came home at the usual time and acted as though nothing had happened. And I said nothing to him. I don't know why I didn't get out of the car and confront him at the motel.

The next week when we were in the car alone, I turned to Ken and said, "How long have you been screwing around?" He said, "Oh, awhile." I said, "How many years?" He said, "A few." I asked if it was someone I knew. Was she young? Was she about my age? Every time I pressed for something definitive, he would be vague. We spent a couple of hours in the car with me letting out my anger. He justified his behavior by saying that for eight years I hadn't wanted sex.

I said, "Well, I've tried to get you to understand that I needed more than sexual encounters." I said I felt like a prostitute to him. I wanted pats on the back and recognition for what I did. I said he must have felt that it was easier for him to have sex with someone else than to make changes in our marriage.

I told him that his Ms. Wonderful didn't have to take care of his dishes or make the dinner or watch the kids. She didn't have to put up with all the shit! All she had to do was listen to him, focus on him, and be screwed by him.

About a week later I asked, "Are you still fooling around?" He said, "No, I stopped."

I do think he stopped. When I asked him why he stopped, he said because he got caught. I don't find his answer much of a comfort.

I just can't seem to let go of my anger at Ken. It has built up over the years. To me the affair is like a crowning blow that says, "I don't care about you. I don't care how much you have done for me."

When I look back and think how much I did in the marriage, I think his affair is such a betrayal. I did the whole ball of wax for 26 years. I have invested too much for too long, both physically and emotionally.

As I see it, there are two stumbling blocks to my getting over my anger. First, Ken only gave up the affair because he was caught. And he has never said he was sorry. I think he feels that he was completely justified. He must believe that the basis of our relationship is sexual.

The other evening I was crying about the sad state of our marriage. He came over and patted me on the shoulder. I said, "I can hardly stand for you to touch me." He said, "Do you hate me that much?" I said, "I can't believe you are saying that. You're focusing on yourself. I don't give a damn whether you think I hate you or not. The point is me. And how badly I'm feeling right now. I need you to focus on ME!"

To Be Or Not To Be Angry

For Marsha to have any kind of resolution with her husband and to move away from her position of feeling "angry righteous," she will need to reconcile within herself that she did what she thought was appropriate. She took care of her husband and her family in a way that she thought fitting. What would be helpful is for her to take comfort in that knowledge and stop focusing on what her husband did not do.

At some point Marsha must also reconcile within herself that, on a subconscious level, she was in collusion with her husband not to get taken care of. Because the more you do in a marriage, the less your partner is likely to do. Marsha, as much as her husband, created the imbalance.

Marsha's decision to reject her husband sexually in order to get his attention was definitely not productive. It did not get her the love and attention she desired.

This couple also seems to have made a covert agreement to avoid intimacy with each other. No one lets a problem go unattended for eight years without getting some psychological payoff.

For Marsha the benefit may have been that she was able to build her anger over the years and view her husband as a jerk. Perhaps this viewpoint confirmed a decision that she made long ago in childhood that men are jerks. Or perhaps it allowed her to play out a recurring pattern from childhood—that no matter how much she does for others she won't be taken care of.

I suspect that Ken's payoff for having an almost sexless marriage was being able to justify having an affair, guilt free.

At this juncture Marsha must decide whether to let go of her anger and hurt and forgive her husband or to continue to go over her lengthy ledger of everything she gave in the marriage and everything her husband did not give.

If she decides to get on with the marriage, she might start by looking at her own behavior to see how she creates distance in this relationship. Certainly she will need to stop obsessing about her husband's affair and making sarcastic comments to him about it. And she will need to work on recognizing some of Ken's good points.

Marsha should also tell Ken that she is interested in making the marriage better. To start, she could tell him that she is willing to make some changes herself, but she also wants some changes from him. She could ask Ken to apologize another hundred times over the next six months for his affair—as a way of acknowledging the emotional pain she has experienced. She could request that Ken give her two or three compliments a day as a way to help her "feel" that he cares about her. These compliments would also go a long way in helping her let go of her anger.

Marsha could decide to see a therapist to reach the goals of resolving her anger and redefining what she expects from the marriage today. She could suggest that Ken go with her for marriage counseling.

And she could make the decision to reintroduce sex into the marriage.

Again . . .

When one partner gives too much and does too much in the relationship, it creates the process whereby the other partner does too little. This imbalance is the third most common reason that couples pull away from each other sexually.

And now a look at the Caretaker in depth.

❧ THE CARETAKER

A Caretaker is a person whose main focus in life is taking care of others. She almost always puts her husband's wants and needs ahead of her own. Because a Caretaker is so focused on others, particularly her husband, her intuitive powers are highly developed. She can walk into a room and instantly feel what is going on. If her husband feels happy, she feels happy. If he is down in the dumps or annoyed about something, she feels uncomfortable and immediately tries to make him happy.

If her husband runs out of orange juice, she'll figure out how she can get to the store sometime that day to pick up another bottle. What is disquieting is that her husband does not expect her to run out and buy him orange juice. And because he hasn't asked her to do him this favor, he's not likely to recognize what she has done.

Because a Caretaker is always focused on others, she often is not aware of what she wants in life or how she feels about things. It's almost as though she is attached to her mate by an invisible umbilical cord that makes her feelings of well-being dependent on her mate's well-being.

A Perfect Caretaker Scene

Liz, another Caretaker, gave this example from her own experience.

> Every Sunday night Don and I watch *Masterpiece Theatre* together. We have been doing this for years. About a quarter to nine I'll go turn on the television set and then I'll go find Don and tell him that it's almost time for Masterpiece. Then I'll sit down and start watching. As it gets closer to show time, I start to feel anxious that Don's going to miss the opening scene.
>
> So I'll yell upstairs, "Come on, Don, it's time." Still no Don. With each passing minute, I feel more anxious because I can't enjoy the show until Don gets there. I want Don there for the opening scene because I think he will enjoy the show more if he sees it from the beginning.
>
> I also know that if the situation were reversed, and if I wasn't there for the opening scene, Don would have no trouble sitting back and enjoying the show.

If you're a Caretaker, you can easily identify with this scenario. Just as the Passive Aggressive subconsciously operates from an "I-count-more-than-you-count" position in life, a Caretaker operates from a "You-count-more-than-I-count" position.

The Caretaker In Action

I recently wrote a script for a video entitled *Closer Encounters* that illustrates how the Caretaker and her husband interact. The scene opens with the Caretaker cutting a piece of chocolate cake. She asks her husband if he would like a piece and he declines.

A few minutes later, the wife walks out on the deck with cake in hand. Her husband says the cake looks delicious, and come to think about it, he would like a piece. Dutifully the Caretaker gives her cake to him and returns to the kitchen to cut herself another piece.

Once the wife is back on the deck and settled in her chair, her husband says, "I wonder what time it's getting to be?" Without a moment's hesitation, she jumps up and checks the time.

Later, when her husband wonders what movies are on TV, the wife puts down her newspaper, finds the movie guide, and reads it to him. This is a Caretaker in action. The sad thing is, neither partner is aware of how much the Caretaker does.

The Caretaker As Controller

Another dynamic between the Caretaker and her mate is that she has a great deal of control in the relationship. After all, if you're the one making most of the decisions and taking most of the responsibility, chances are you're going to do most things your way.

You may be the one who has to decide that it's time to wallpaper the dining room, and you may be the one who has to go to the store and pick out the wallpaper, and you may even be the one who hangs it. But you also get to make all the decisions.

I remember years ago complaining to my husband about always being responsible for the Christmas shopping. He responded that he would be more than happy to go with me, or, if I wanted, he would split the list and do half the shopping. What I found disturbing was that I *didn't want* him to do any of the shopping. What I learned about myself was that I wanted to choose the gifts. I also wanted to decide how much money would be spent on each person. I wanted the control. Even today I wrestle with myself when my husband suggests going to buy a birthday gift for one of our children. It's not the job I want so much but the control.

Another way a Caretaker tries to control is by asking her husband to do something; then, before he has a chance to do it, she does it. She can't wait, for fear he's not going to do it. This, too, keeps the relationship off balance, with her doing more and him doing less.

A good illustration of this recently appeared in the comic strip *Blondie*.

In the first frame, Dagwood's secretary tells him that Blondie has called to remind him not to forget the fish for tonight's dinner. In the next frame the office boy reminds him. In the next, his boss reminds him. Then his receptionist tells him. As he is leaving the office, two other people remind him, "Don't forget the fish."

As Dagwood walks into the fish store, who should be there but Blondie. As Dagwood looks perplexed, Blondie chirps, "Hi, honey; I was afraid you'd forget about the fish."*

---

* From *Blondie*, Copyright © 1989, King Features Syndicate. All rights reserved. Reprinted with special permission of King Features Syndicate, Inc.

An Advice Giver

Another trait of the Caretaker is her tendency to be an advice giver. In other words, the Caretaker, like her Corrector sister, enjoys telling other people what to do. This fits with her secret desire to run the show.

If a Caretaker has a personal crisis and needs support, however, she has difficulty asking others for help. It's almost as though she sees her need for support as a failing or an imperfection. Besides, admitting that she can't handle everything on her own means that she has to give up some control.

Unfortunately, when a Caretaker takes the risk and asks someone for help or support, she is often given the brush-off, as though she couldn't possibly have any problems or need help.

The Caretaker and Sex

Caretakers handle sex in their marriage in a wide variety of ways. Some Caretakers carry their need to please right into the marital bed. They rarely refuse their husbands' sexual advances, and if their husbands reach orgasm, they feel they have done their job. In fact, many Caretakers are content simply to masturbate their husbands to orgasm, expecting nothing for themselves.

As one Caretaker I interviewed said,

> We're lying in bed and he reaches out and touches me in a way that lets me know he wants sex. Immediately, I go into action. I rise up, lean over him, and start taking off his pajamas, just like in the movies. All the while he lies there with his head on the pillow. If I want

him to do something to me, I have to stop fooling around with him. Only then does he become active. I definitely orchestrate the whole thing.

Other Caretakers report that sex is the one area where they expect their husbands to do the approaching and take the lead. Frequently this stance is the result of early scripting, which says that it's a man's job to be the aggressor sexually.

Caretakers, particularly those in their 20s and 30s, have said that this is one area where they take themselves into consideration. They approach their husbands when they want sex. They expect their husbands to approach them. They do not have sex if they don't want it. And they expect to be sexually satisfied.

The one constant that I have found is that because a Caretaker gives too much in too many areas of her marriage, she almost always starts to feel resentful and taken advantage of. This resentment is often evidenced by critical comments, low-level depression, and less and less interest in approaching her partner sexually or responding to his advances.

❧ "I TRY TO MAKE PEOPLE HAPPY SO THEY WILL LOVE ME"

Although Karen's husband had left her a week before our interview, I decided to include the following story because it is so typical of the Caretaker. Karen's story may encourage other Caretakers to focus less on their partners and more on themselves.

Karen's Story

I always thought that it was my responsibility as a wife and mother to make everyone happy. It was my job to keep things running smoothly, to make sure everyone had clean underwear and everyone got where they were going. If my husband popped a button on his shirt, he would say, "This button came off my shirt." And I would automatically say, "Do you need it now or later?" If he needed it then, I would drop everything and sew it on.

In the beginning, all my caretaking wasn't a big job. But then we had children and bought a house, and all of a sudden my responsibilities got bigger. I ran the household. I paid all the bills. I made claims to the insurance companies and updated our policies. There was going to the pediatrician, going to PTA meetings, making costumes for the kids for Halloween. My time got used up. I kept taking on more and more responsibilities. Ed didn't take on more. I guess he didn't think about it. And heck, I didn't think about it either.

I did all the shopping for anything that needed to be purchased. Ed only liked to go to the hardware store, where he could poke around. I bought all his clothes. I bought all the gifts for his relatives and for his secretaries. He wouldn't have given them a gift if I hadn't bought them. You see, I wanted them to be happy, too.

At the same time I was doing all the shopping for everyone, Ed never spent any time picking out things for me that I liked. One year for Christmas I gave him a beautiful briefcase. I spent an enormous amount of time going from luggage shop to luggage shop looking for just the right one. I knew he liked a certain depth, a certain color, and a certain type of leather. I have always paid attention to what pleased him.

What did he give me? A silly, see-through orange teddy. This is definitely not me. If he had wanted to please me, he would have given me a classic, full-length black negligee, not an orange teddy with ruffles.

I would try to please him by pretending that I liked his gifts. He always gave me what he wanted.

I must say when I shopped for him I got a great amount of pleasure. I feel good when I make other people happy. I'm known for giving just the right gift. I think if you're tuned into someone, you pick out the right gift for that person.

When someone is unhappy, I think about how I can change things so he will be happy—even if it's at a great sacrifice to me. I don't want to be an uncaring person, but I need to find a happy medium.

Our relationship started to break down when I went back to work. I had less time, so I had to give up something. Sadly, I gave up every shred of personal time I had. I gave up playing racquetball. I gave up sculpting. I now realize that was probably the worst thing that I could do. I gave up any outlet I had to reduce my stress and keep myself on an even keel.

I'd rush home and start fixing dinner after working nine hours. Everyone would start telling me what they needed. The kids would want certain clothes for the next day. Ed would ask if I had stopped by the safe deposit box. In fourteen years every trip that was made to the safe deposit box, with one exception, was mine.

Nobody ever put anything in the dishwasher. Sometimes I'd say, "Hey, it would help me if you put the dishes in the dishwasher." How silly of me to say that, as if their dishes were my responsibility. Sometimes I still catch myself thinking, "Oh heck, it's easier to do it myself."

I've suddenly realized I've sacrificed everything over the years. I gave up my time, I sacrificed monetarily. It was not that my family ever said, "Okay, you be our slave, and we'll play and get plenty of rest." But that's how it ended up.

I never could figure out why my husband was angry with me. I always tried so hard. Maybe he was angry because if one person does too much and the other doesn't reciprocate, the person who doesn't do much starts feeling guilty. I now see that my doing everything was being too much in control. When I'm doing everything I'm making all the decisions. In retrospect, I think I probably made him feel worthless.

I think it all goes back to the beginning of our relationship. Our roles were already established by the way we grew up. I needed to take care of someone, and Ed needed to be taken care of.

My mom is seventy-three and still fixes my dad's lunch. My dad is retired. My mom will say to me, "I have to get off the phone now and make your dad's lunch." My dad is so passive.

I decided I would never marry a passive man. I wanted it fifty-fifty. When we first met, Ed said, "In my marriage I want to be the president and I want my wife to be the vice-president." That sounded great to me. I wanted someone to take the major responsibilities. I wanted someone to take care of me. But it didn't work out that way because in spite of what he said, Ed was passive.

I try to make people happy so they will love me. So they will fill some of my emotional needs. When I was a little girl, the way I got attention and love in my family was by achieving, getting an award, getting an A. I have always felt that doing things for others would get me love and attention.

I don't know what I need from other people. I'm forty-two years old and I don't think I've ever really thought about what I need. It makes me sad. I've taken care of people more than half my life. And I've waited more than half my life to be taken care of.

ಒ IF YOU ARE A CARETAKER

If you are like Karen, always waiting to be taken care of, decide today to stop waiting and start taking better care of yourself.

Block off one hour for yourself per day. It will be difficult, and you won't always take an hour; but the more you work at it, the better your chances are of really learning to focus on yourself.

If you've always wanted to learn ballroom dancing, go to a studio and sign up. You do not need your husband to go with you. If you enjoy collecting antiques, take some time every week to go antique hunting. If you have a desire to learn about art, do it.

If it were your husband or your children who wanted to explore something new, you would have no trouble encouraging and supporting them. So encourage yourself.

You should also start saying to yourself roughly 3,000 times a day, "I'm a good person when I take care of myself. I'm a good person when I take care of myself." You can repeat this affirmation as you are taking a shower, or blow-drying your hair, or sitting at an intersection waiting for the light to turn green. After a few months, you'll come to believe it.

Certainly people need to take care of each other. And you need to continue to take care of your husband. But he needs to take care of you, too. If you do too much, you are responsible for setting in motion the dynamic that he will do too little.

Remember, if you're a Caretaker, you already know how to fulfill your partner's wants and needs. So you're halfway there. Now all you have to do is learn to make yourself count.

❧ IF YOUR MATE IS A CARETAKER

If you are married to a Caretaker, the best way to get your wife to feel more positive about you and to want to have sex with you is to take better care of her both physically and emotionally.

Start by making a list of all you do and a list of all she does. Then revise those lists with the intention of balancing them and making them more equal. Don't forget all those unsolicited hugs and backrubs and compliments that she gives you. Don't forget the hidden chores, such as going through a child's drawer every few months to remove all the clothes that are too small. Don't forget all the arranging and cooking she does before a family dinner or outing.

Another important thing to be aware of—how do you inadvertently invite your wife to take care of you? Do you say such things as, "A bowl of ice cream would sure taste good about now," and expect her to jump up and get it for you? Do you casually mention that it's been some time since you've had your mother to your home and expect your wife to invite her and entertain her while you sit passively and watch television? Do you get quiet and withdrawn when your wife tells you she's thinking of going to a movie with a friend, so that she'll stay home with you instead? Do you want her to have oral sex on you while refusing to reciprocate? When you have sex, do you often lie there and let her masturbate you to orgasm, but never return the favor?

All these behaviors are subtly designed to insure that she will take care of you, instead of your taking care of yourself or taking care of her. If you're guilty of doing any of these things, you should change your behavior.

❧ BALANCING THE SEE-SAW MEANS MORE SEX

Although most marriages are not equal, there could be a better balance in most relationships if both partners shared more of the chores and parenting and took equal responsibility for the emotional health of the relationship.

Research has shown that where there is equity in a relationship, the partners have more respect for each other, there is more camaraderie, the couple is happier, and there is more emotional and physical intimacy.

CHAPTER FIVE

THE PASSIVE TAKER MAN

In this chapter you will meet several people who have Passive Taker personalities.

The Passive Taker is a person who does not seem to be aware of his own wants or needs; nor does he seem aware of others' wants and needs. Although a nice, easy-going guy who is usually willing to help out if assigned a task, he rarely organizes or plans ahead or takes responsibility in the marriage. And he rarely initiates sex.

Because a Passive Taker generally does not initiate sex, he inadvertently shifts the responsibility for sex to his wife. If she is willing to approach him, they will probably have sex. Frequently, however, the wife of a Passive Taker will start to feel resentful and rejected because her husband does not pursue her. And as these feelings of hurt and resentment build, she will often give up pursuing him for sex.

This sets into motion the following dynamic:

When one partner is passive and does not initiate sex, it creates the process whereby the entire burden to initiate sex falls on the other partner. This imbalance is a fourth reason why couples do not have sex more frequently.

❧ THE CASE OF THE MISSING LIBIDO

Now meet Barb and Jack, a couple in their early thirties. They have been married for eight years and have two small children.

Barb's Story

We have sex maybe every four to six months. I used to complain all the time about not having sex. I think my complaining started because I wanted Jack's love and attention and he wouldn't give it to me. So I reacted by telling him what he should be doing and how he should be acting. I'd say, "Men are supposed to have a sex drive. What's the matter with you? How come you don't desire me?"

Nothing seems to get Jack interested in sex. If I get dolled up, if I put on a sexy nightgown, or if he enters the bathroom when I'm in the bathtub, it has no effect. He has never given me any indication of desiring sex, except when we were first married. I don't approach him because I think he should approach me. I think having sex with me is not worth the effort for him. It is easier for him to masturbate. He confessed that he masturbates a couple of times a week. When he told me I was shocked. I was devastated.

I've often thought, Why have I let so little sex go on for so long? I think it's because I don't enjoy sex itself. I don't reach orgasm. I want communication and attention. So I've been willing to do without the actual act.

When I did push Jack for sex, we'd have sex. Afterwards, he'd make a promise to change and approach me more and show me more love. His attention would last for a few days, and then he would start neglecting me again. Then I'd start nagging. He'd say, "How can I show love to you? All you do is nag and bitch." I accepted his excuse—because I did nag and bitch.

I'd watch Oprah Winfrey and Donahue and all the shows, anything that had something on sex. I'd read articles in magazines and think, Is there something wrong with me? Is there something wrong with him? Then I'd discuss it with him. After one of these shows, the pressure would really be on, so we'd have sex. This would satisfy me for awhile, but then there would be no sex again for another four to six months.

Even when we have sex, Jack's passive. He doesn't kiss me much. There isn't much foreplay. It takes all of ten to fifteen minutes. He gets an erection. We have intercourse. He's on top, then we flip over and I'm on top. He has an orgasm, then he goes to sleep. One time he said, "Too bad that you didn't come." But he doesn't do anything to help me.

He sits on the couch every night watching television. It doesn't matter what he watches. It doesn't matter what we have for dinner. It just doesn't matter! He doesn't criticize, he doesn't compliment . . . but worst of all, he doesn't notice. I've tried to figure out over the years what's important to him, what matters to him. It's like he lives in his own world.

Nothing seems to faze him. Whether the house is a mess or straightened up, he doesn't comment either way. We could be watching the World Series, the last inning, the score tied, and he'd yawn, check his watch, and go to bed. I could walk by the television set with nothing on and he wouldn't notice.

If I suddenly asked him to close his eyes during a conversation, he wouldn't be able to say if I was wearing my contacts or my glasses. Once I had my hair cut and permed. I looked like Shirley Temple and *he didn't notice!* I don't think he ever looks at me, come to think about it.

We went to Jack's parents' house for a family party recently, and he sat in a chair and just stared into space. He doesn't get involved with people. I waved my arms at him to get his attention. He smiled and said, "I'm tired." Later he went into the other room and read the newspaper. Then I saw him at the bookshelf looking through their books. One of our daughters came up to him and asked him for a drink. He said, "Just go take a drink out of one of the cups you find." I almost died! Jack always takes the easy way out.

When I get mad at him, he just doesn't understand why I'm angry. I think he decides the incident is not worth being angry over. He listens to me go on and on, but he does not react to my anger. When I finally wear myself down and become quiet, he shrugs, and then he defends himself. He says, "It's not the way you think." But he doesn't explain.

He often rents movies that we've already seen. One time he changed the channel on the television set when there was a roomful of people watching a movie. This is why I criticize him. I point out the world and what is going on around him. Sometimes when I correct him, I also feel like I'm taking care of him, that I'm being helpful to him.

I say, "I want you to put fertilizer on the grass . . . the house needs painting . . . the roof is leaking." I become the taskmaster. I think he feels resentful because I'm always giving orders. But things have to be done. I've treated him like a baby for a long time. That's probably why the man has avoided me. I am always correcting.

For many years I saw Jack's laid-back attitude as a good quality. He's so easygoing. But at this point I wish he would take a stand, have an opinion, share with me, make love to me, tell me something he likes, something he doesn't like. Maybe he's afraid I'd use the information against him. Who knows?

The Opposite of Love Is Not Hate, but Indifference

Although, in the beginning of the marriage, Jack seemed like an idyllic mate, as with most relationships with a Passive Taker, this one has deteriorated over time. Rarely will one partner be willing to make all the decisions and take all the responsibility without feeling resentful.

The other reason this type of marriage runs into trouble is that the partner who is doing almost all the work to keep the relationship going is rarely affirmed. As Barb said: "He doesn't criticize, he doesn't compliment . . . but worst of all, he doesn't notice."

Although Barb claims that she is not all that interested in sex, this seems doubtful. Whenever Barb and Jack have sex, it seems to be the direct result of her badgering him to approach her. Perhaps her interest in sex has more to do with needing attention than needing sexual release. Or perhaps her interest has to do with the need that most people have to be able to say to themselves that sex is a part of their marriage.

What Barb might do is to make the decision to approach Jack—instead of pushing him to approach her. This is a difficult decision for many women to make, as many women receive the message in childhood that a man should do the approaching. However, making the decision to approach your Passive Taker is one way to keep sex in the marriage.

⮞ THE PASSIVE TAKER

As described earlier, a Passive Taker is someone who is only vaguely conscious of the world around him. He is not aware of his own or others' wants and needs. He is a nice, even-tempered guy. He rarely gets angry. He is usually willing to go along with whatever others suggest. He is easily pleased. He seems content doing almost anything.

The main problem with this personality type is that the Passive Taker discounts himself and what he wants in life. He also discounts his partner and what she wants. Passive Taker simply does not take responsibility for himself; nor does he take responsibility in the relationship. He doesn't make decisions, he doesn't plan, he doesn't notice what's going on around him. As a result, everything becomes the responsibility of the Passive Taker's wife. Or, as Barb so aptly put it, she becomes the "taskmaster." It is up to her to decide when to paint the house, whether the children should have braces, and if and when to have sex.

How Passive Can You Get?

How passive a Passive Taker can actually become is evidenced in the following two incidents.

The first happened a few years ago when I was out to dinner with friends. As we were ordering, the waiter asked one of the men what kind of salad dressing he would like. Without hesitation, this man turned and looked to his wife. It was his salad, but in typical passive taker fashion, he expected her to tell him what kind of salad dressing he should order.

Another woman had decided to have her husband's favorite rocking chair reupholstered. First she asked him if he wanted to go with her to pick out the fabric. He said no. She then asked if he wanted to see the material and put his stamp of approval on it before she actually ordered it. No, he said, he trusted her judgment. She called the upholstery company and had them pick up the chair. The chair was gone for four weeks, and her husband never mentioned that the chair was missing. "A chair that he sat in nightly for fifteen years," she said. Finally the chair came back with its new fabric, and even then he never made a comment about it.

Sex and the Passive Taker

Of the four personality types, it is the Passive Taker who is the least likely to initiate sex. It is also the Passive Taker who is most likely to be passive during sex. Again, the way the Passive Taker handles sex reflects the way he deals with life in general.

If Passive Taker's wife doesn't initiate sex—because she believes that it is a man's job to do the approaching or she thinks she already takes too much responsibility in too many other areas of the marriage—sex isn't going to happen.

If, on the other hand, the wife is willing to initiate, the couple probably will have sex. Remember, Passive Takers usually go along with the program. They just don't initiate.

Another dynamic is that, because the Passive Taker gives his wife little attention, sexually or otherwise, she often feels that there must be something wrong with her. As time goes by, she finds it more and more difficult to make demands sexually. In fact, some women have said that asking for sex becomes an embarrassment.

Following is an interview with another woman, Ellie (38), who is married to a Passive Taker. This couple has sex a little more than the last couple we met because, as Ellie says . . .

&. "HE STILL TURNS ME ON PHYSICALLY. . . IT'S JUST THAT I DON'T FEEL GOOD ABOUT HIM EMOTIONALLY"

Ellie's Story

To the best of my recollection, we have sex about every couple of months. The reason we don't make love more is that our marriage is falling apart. I want sex, but not under these circumstances. So many things are lousy in our marriage that sex isn't appealing. I'm not sure I love David anymore. I know that I don't respect him.

If I ask him whether he wants to go out, he says, "Um, I was thinking about it." But he waits for me to make the decision. He qualifies almost every answer he gives me. It's always a "maybe" or an "I guess" or an "I don't know" answer. He makes me crazy.

He rarely comes up with anything to do. He might say, "I think I'd like to see the ocean." But he would never say, "Let's go to the ocean this summer." He denies his emotions. He says he's not angry, but his body language says he is. He doesn't stand up for his own ideas. He is not willing to take me on. He doesn't say what he wants.

I started pulling away sexually years ago. I just stopped pursuing him. And he never approaches me. He waits for me to approach him.

If David would just pursue sex in any way, if he tried to coax me a bit, more than likely we would make love more often because he still turns me on physically. That's the reason why we have sex every few months. It's just that I don't feel good about him emotionally.

🐟 LIVING WITH A PASSIVE TAKER

One of the best ways to start feeling better about your Passive Taker is to stop trying to anticipate all his wants and needs.

For example, if you ask him if he would like tea or coffee with dinner and he responds, "Whatever," do not go ahead and make this decision for him. Instead, say, "When you decide, I'll pour." You don't have to be sarcastic, but avoid making decisions that he should be making.

If you see that he is running out of his favorite cereal, do not pick up another box unless he specifically asks you to do so. This approach might seem hard-hearted at first, but the more you automatically take care of a Passive Taker, the less responsibility he will take for himself and the less he will take care of you.

Remember, if you continually give your partner recognition, whether it be compliments or complaints, and you continue to make all the decisions and do all the chores, you set the stage for your mate to do little and to give little back to you emotionally.

As for sex with a Passive Taker, it's important to make a decision that if you enjoy sex you will take responsibility and approach your partner.

One way to get a Passive Taker to learn to approach you is to get in bed and snuggle up next to him and say, "Okay, your turn to start fooling around." If you have to, take his hand and help him get started.

If he is passive during lovemaking, tell him right at the time what you want him to do. If you find that you're too shy to verbalize what you want, show him by taking his hand and guiding him along. Simply hoping that your partner will take care of you will not get you taken care of.

I frequently tell a woman who is married to a full-fledged Passive Aggressive or Passive Taker that one way to take care of yourself is to take responsibility for those things in the relationship that mean the most to you.

For example, if you feel strongly that the kitchen must be neat and tidy at all times, take on this chore and negotiate with your husband to take responsibility for something that doesn't matter quite so much to you, such as keeping the garage clean. Although it's an annoyance, you can survive if the garage never gets cleaned.

The same principle holds true for sex. If you want sex, *approach*. Although you may not feel as good as you would feel if he approached you, it's better than no sex in the relationship.

CHAPTER SIX

BICKERING AND FIGHTING FOR CONTROL

At a seminar recently I was discussing the enormous range of issues that people find to bicker and fight over, when I asked the audience what issues they were presently arguing about. One woman volunteered that she and her husband had had a disagreement that very morning over what kind of coffee pot to purchase. She wanted a percolator, "which makes hot coffee," and he wanted "one of those coffee makers where you pour the water in the top—and out comes very lukewarm coffee."

Another woman said that she and her husband had been disagreeing for a week about when to plant the tulip bulbs. She thought that they should do it right away, whereas he wanted to wait a few more weeks. She went on to explain that she was afraid that the ground would freeze and then they wouldn't get their bulbs in this year—just like the previous winter when he insisted on waiting too long.

It's clear from both of these women's comments that they were in the throes of a power struggle. Notice how both of them presented their side more favorably than their husbands'. The first woman didn't want "lukewarm coffee." The second woman made sure we all knew that they had not gotten their bulbs in last year because of her husband.

A man now volunteered. He said that when he and his wife get in the car to go somewhere, they usually disagree about whether the radio should be on. Usually he'll get in the car and turn on the radio. Then his wife gets in and turns it off.

"What do you do when she turns the radio off?" I asked.

"I turn it back on," he said.

"How often do you do this?" I queried.

"Every time we get in the car," he responded.

This man's wife was also there, so I asked her about not liking the radio. She said, "I like the radio fine, but I think that when you're in the car, it's a good time to talk."

At that point her husband piped up and said disgustedly, "That's right. She always wants to have a talk."

Now most of the couples in the audience were smiling. They were identifying with the power struggle of the wife wanting to talk and the husband not wanting to talk.

I then asked this fellow what these talks were generally about. He said that they were usually about him, and how he needed to improve on something.

On one level this couple is struggling over control of the radio. On another level they are struggling over the wife's need to talk about what she wants her husband to change, versus the husband's desire not to hear what his wife finds objectionable. The issues: Who will decide what is going to happen in the car, who will decide how the husband will behave, and who ultimately has the control in the marriage.

Certainly life without any differences of opinion or resistance from one's partner would be boring. At the same time . . . too many power struggles over the way a couple will handle things are definite deterrents to making love.

❧ WHEN BICKERING GETS IN THE WAY OF SEX

Jerry is seventy-one and Roberta is sixty-six. For both, this is their second marriage. They have just celebrated their twelfth anniversary.

Jerry's Side

Up until about two years ago, we had a great sex life. Then we started bickering, and the bickering has gotten worse. In the last three months we have had sex only once or twice. Before that it was once or twice a week. Roberta says she can't have sex with me as long as we're arguing.

One of our problems is that we can't agree on where to be buried. I plan to be buried next to my first wife. I'm doing this for my children. I have a space for Roberta next to me on the other side. But she doesn't want to be buried there.

We constantly disagree about the temperature in the house. She wants the thermostat set at sixty-four degrees winter and summer. She's always too hot and I'm always freezing. She says, "Put on a sweater." This upsets our sex life because it gets me upset. How would you like to walk around in your house and be freezing all the time?

When she's in the car she turns the heater on full blast. Her temperature is always fluctuating. In the house she's hot and I freeze. In the car she freezes and I'm frying. In the car it's hard to breathe because she has so much heat blasting me in the face.

I can't talk to her in the morning because she likes to sleep in and then have breakfast. She won't talk to me before she has breakfast. I have at least ten things to go over with her, but I always have to wait.

Another thing that keeps us from having sex is that I feel I can't do anything to please her. She thinks I'm doing things I shouldn't be doing for a man my age. She tells me I shouldn't get on a ladder. She doesn't want me to carry suitcases. She doesn't want me to lift anything. She's always asking me what time I went to bed. When I say, "One o'clock," she tells me that's too late.

She is a nervous wreck in the car. She is forever telling me where to park, where to turn. There's this constant bitching about my driving. And I'm a damn good driver! I turn on the radio and she says, "Can't we have peace and quiet?" I get so aggravated with her that I don't approach her. If I did, she wouldn't respond anyway. And she won't approach me.

When we go to a restaurant she asks the waiter a million questions because of her cholesterol. She wants to know how the food is cooked. What kind of oil is it cooked in? Do they use salt? What kind of salt? Is it cooked in butter?

My cholesterol count is great. My blood pressure is great. My triglycerides are perfect. But she still says I should cut down on my fats because it could be a problem.

She's a great dresser. The other day I said, "That jacket looks great. Is that new?" She snapped back, "I've had it for over two years." That shut me up. I can't remember her clothes. She's got zillions.

I had a jacket on the other day and she said, "How old is that jacket?" I said, "A few years." She said, "Give it away." So I went and put on another one. When she saw me, she said, "Give that one away too." So I put on another one. Maybe I should appreciate the fact that she tells me not to wear certain things, but it's criticism. It aggravates me.

I bought myself some new shoes the other day. She told me, "Those are the clumsiest-looking shoes I've ever seen." I seldom criticize what she wears, but she sure criticizes what I wear.

I'm sports-minded. When we first got married, we went to the football and hockey games together. Now she won't attend any of these events. We used to play golf. She says I make her play too difficult a course, so she won't play anymore. We don't have any rapport. We never watch television together. She doesn't like to watch sporting events. She watches that gal Oprah Winfrey every day.

When we have sex, it's nice. I sometimes have trouble maintaining an erection. Recently I've had trouble ejaculating. You know, it's my age. She says, "Don't worry about it." I use a vibrator on her.

Oral sex—now that's great. She has it on me. I have it on her. I know she likes it.

Sometimes when we are in bed she says, "Have you washed?" I say, "No." She says, "I told you to wash before you come to bed." I say, "Why should I wash when nothing happens?" If I know we are going to have sex, I wash.

After sex she doesn't want me to put my pajamas back on. But I can't sleep nude. After about an hour I put on my pajamas because I'm freezing.

Roberta's Side

When we first got married, we had sex every night and every morning. Now that's a lot! That went on for a number of years. About four years ago it wasn't as often, maybe three times a week. It has now gotten to the point where we almost never have sex because there is some difficulty between us almost every day. So I don't approach him. I enjoy sex, but I don't want to have sex with him when we're not getting along.

He thinks he's in charge of the heat and the air conditioning and a million other things. If a repairman comes out to do anything, Jerry has to be there. He doesn't trust anyone to do the job right. He wants to tell them what to do and how to do it. Yesterday I wanted the ice machine hooked up. He said, "The maid said we don't need any more ice." I said, "Since when is the maid running the house?" He said, "You're too sarcastic. I can't talk to you."

If we go marketing together and I stop to read a label or to talk with someone, he says, "Come on, we came in here to market." He wants to tell me how long I can shop.

He won't let me take his cleaning to the dry cleaners. I wouldn't do it right. He thinks he is the only one who can do it correctly. He is so bogged down with work because he won't let anyone else help him. He is always working at his desk. He is never finished. He will sit up working until 1:00 or 2:00 in the morning.

Before he goes to bed he has to write notes for what he is going to do tomorrow. He also scratches off all the items he has done for that day. It drives me crazy.

If we talk, it's about what he has to do. If I say, "Let me read you something," he says, "How long is it?"

If I say, "What did you think of the movie?" he says, "It was good." But he doesn't say anything more. I enjoy talking about the plot. I like to analyze. I'm people-oriented. I like to discuss what's happening in the world, what's going on in our families' lives, our children's lives. But Jerry just doesn't discuss things. He is so busy fixing things and working at his desk that he doesn't see what a lovely day it is, what a beautiful world we live in.

If I have a problem with one of my children, he's unsympathetic. He doesn't sit down and help me talk it out or try to make me feel better. I have trouble sleeping. He isn't sympathetic. One of my best friends died last week. She had been sick for a long time. Yesterday he said, "Now you'll be better. You can return to normal." He doesn't seem to understand that I need time to grieve.

When I'm sick, he's kind in the beginning. But if I'm sick too long, he gets angry. After a day or two he says, "It's time to get up now. You're well." He wants things back to normal.

He wants me to do things for him, but always the way he wants it done. The problem is I won't do everything his way. And that makes him mad. Boy, does that make him mad!

I've tried to tell him that the kitchen is my domain. If I throw out anything in the refrigerator, he has a stroke. He volunteers to go to the market, so I'll ask him to buy a certain thing. If it's on sale, he'll come home with the item. Otherwise he won't buy it. When I go, I buy what I want. When he goes, he buys what he wants. Now isn't that ridiculous!

He's a sweet man, but he can't stand it if I tell him how to do something. He will never admit that I'm right about anything. He wants to run the whole show. He wants everything his way—so our sex life is suffering.

A Question of Compromise

Some of Jerry and Roberta's disagreements, like the one over where Jerry is going to be buried, can be solved only by one of them getting his or her way. But many of their disagreements could be solved through compromise.

Roberta might compromise by turning up the thermostat a little and having a few fans that she could switch on and adjust in her direction. She could compromise by occasionally attending a sporting event or watching television with her husband. Roberta could also decide to stop trying to control her husband by making helpful suggestions about what he should eat or when he should come to bed. Although Roberta might argue that her suggestions are made only because she is concerned for Jerry's health, they are also attempts to get Jerry to live his life as she thinks he should live it.

Another important factor is that Jerry does not view Roberta's suggestions as helpful and caring. Nor does he feel closer to her for making them. And Roberta's insistence on making them is messing up their sex life.

Jerry, too, could do some compromising in this marriage. When Roberta asks him to buy a certain item at the market, he could buy it despite the price. He could make the decision that no matter what foods his wife throws away, he will say nothing. Perhaps the biggest compromise for Jerry would be to sit with Roberta and talk with her two or three hours a week. He could also decide to listen attentively when she wants to read him an article, even if it is on diet and cholesterol.

Neither Jerry nor Roberta is wrong in the way each wants to live his or her life. They are certainly butting heads, however, because each of them thinks that his or her way is the right way. And each of them expects the other to change.

Another source of conflict in this marriage is that Jerry is very task-oriented. He likes doing projects and being busy. Roberta, on the other hand, is more people-oriented. She likes to discuss and analyze. She also appreciates sitting back and relaxing and enjoying the day.

Jerry seems to accept his declining sexual power and to have a good understanding of the part age plays in a man's ability both to maintain an erection and ejaculate. Roberta also seems quite accepting of the whole thing. Her comment, "Don't worry about it," suggests she isn't uptight about Jerry's slowed-down sexual response.

I think that since this couple has also given themselves permission to enjoy sex orally, the pressure is off Jerry to maintain a firm erection.

One could speculate that this couple's bickering is an avenue to avoid sex because of Jerry's slowed-down sexual response, but in this case it seems unlikely. Here are two people who are both intelligent, strong-willed, and capable, and who both want to be in charge and tell the other what to do.

❧ "I TURN HER DOWN AT LEAST FIFTY PERCENT OF THE TIME"

Now meet Mike, a man who openly admits to turning his wife down sexually at least half the time.

Mike's withholding sex seems to be an attempt to balance or equalize the power between him and his wife—because his perception is that he does more for his wife and their relationship than she does. His withholding of sex might even be viewed as a retaliatory maneuver. As he says, "I don't think she does enough for me, so I refuse to have sex with her."

Mike and Sue have been in their relationship for four years. They have been married for two years. They have no children. He is 34 and she is 29. They have sex on an average of once a week. Mike says that he's satisfied with the amount of sex they have, but he knows that Sue would like to make love more often.

Mike's Story

Sex doesn't play as big a part in the relationship for me as it does for Sue. If we have an argument, whether we resolve it or not, having sex is a resolution for Sue. It is a type of healing. If I want things to get better between the two of us after an argument, I initiate sex. Sex seems to be a way to reassure Sue that everything is okay. It doesn't solve the particular problem, but it's comforting.

Generally, either of us will initiate sex. If I initiate, Sue rarely refuses, unless she's really tired or she physically doesn't feel well. On the other hand, I admit, I do turn her down at least fifty percent of the time.

Why do I turn her down? Because I believe I do more in the relationship than she does. I don't think she does enough for me, so I refuse to have sex with her. Basically, I think I'm a more caring person than she is. I buy her presents. I fix the coffee maker at night so she will have coffee the next morning. I take care of all the travel arrangements. When we have sex, I have to take care of her first. She wants to reach orgasm before we have intercourse.

We share housework and marketing. We also have a cleaning lady. If we're having a dinner party, I make all the calls inviting everyone. I do it because I want to know who's going to come. If someone can't come, then I'll know and I'll invite someone else. She will put off the calling till the last minute. I make sure certain programs are recorded on our video recorder. I can't count on her to do it. She says, "I couldn't do it the way you want it done." I resent that.

I also get aggravated at her because she does not want my suggestions. She perceives comments such as, "You've missed one of your belt loops," or, "Your hair needs fixing in the back," as negative. Also, she doesn't want any suggestions about how to handle her job. So I also withhold compliments from her. If she can't accept my suggestions, I'm not going to give her compliments.

Complimenting my wife is also difficult because she wants it so much. She wants me to tell her I love her twenty times a day. To her, saying I love you is a cure-all.

She perceives me as being critical of her body. I'm careful not to say anything but, "You look great. You look thin." She won't walk naked in front of me. She won't take off her nightgown except under the covers. She says she's shy. I think that's ludicrous.

When we're not intimate, we blame it on our schedules. We say we're too tired. She gets up early and goes to bed early. I get up later and go to bed later. Monday through Thursday there is a possibility that we'll have sex if I go to bed early. But generally we put it off till the weekend.

If we go out on Friday and Saturday night, we're tired by the time we get home. Sometimes we work in sex on Saturday afternoon before we go out. Tiredness does play a part in our not having sex that's for sure. But mostly it's because we're not getting along.

Balancing the Power

In many ways this marriage is a reversal of the typical hus-band and wife roles. In this case it is the man who is ir-ritated that his wife doesn't take better care of him and the woman who feels as though no matter what she does, it's never quite right. Because Mike doesn't think Sue takes care of him as he takes care of her, he sees Sue as having the power and control in the relationship. As a way to equalize Sue's power, Mike withholds sex half the time.

Another power struggle this couple has is over the kind of feedback Mike is allowed to give Sue. Sue refuses to hear suggestions from Mike about her job, and Mike retaliates by withholding compliments.

One technique Mike could use to improve the marriage is to listen when Sue talks about her job without making any suggestions as to what she might do differently. So often in this hurry-up world we live in, couples do not listen thoroughly to one another's problems. Instead, a partner will come up with all kinds of solutions for solving the problem, instead of listening to his mate talk.

In talking about a problem, people are often able to dis-sipate feelings connected with the issue, and frequently they are able to see how they might solve it themselves. If one mate gives a lot of unsolicited advice, the other will feel pressure to follow some of the suggestions and guilty if she chooses not to go along with them. If the mate who has got-ten the suggestions doesn't use any of them, she is also not as likely to bring the issue up again, which closes off one potential avenue of discussion.

One thing that Sue might decide to do is to start giving Mike more attention. She might make a pact with herself to give Mike five hugs and five compliments a day, as well as a small surprise each week, such as a special bar of soap or a paperback book. This would certainly make Mike feel that he is important and special. And chances are he would be less likely to withhold sex.

Mike is setting a dangerous precedent by turning Sue down as often as he does. As time goes on, it's likely that Sue will become more resentful and even less prone to compliment Mike and do nice things for him. And if he repeatedly turns her down, she eventually will stop approaching.

❧ WHEN HE DOESN'T DO WHAT SHE WANTS IN BED, SHE GOES PASSIVE

Meet Abby, a woman who understands fully how she and her husband struggle for control in their relationship.

Abby and her husband, Luke, are in their mid-fifties. They have been married for twelve years, she for the first time and he for the second.

Abby's Story

Sometimes we have sex one or two times a week, and sometimes it's only once a month. Sex is sometimes painful because I'm going through menopause and I don't lubricate like I used to. I think Luke knows that sex is uncomfortable sometimes, but I also think he feels put down by it, like I'm making an excuse. There can only be a certain amount of foreplay before it becomes uncomfortable for me. He wants me to have orgasm. It's part of his thing. When I tell him I'm getting uncomfortable and why don't we just go ahead and have intercourse, he either says, "Oh, okay," in a disappointed manner or he gets up and says, "I'm going to take a shower." He has a hard time with me saying what I need or want.

Since the beginning of our marriage, we have had this terrible problem—who is going to be in control. We'll be making love and what he's doing isn't satisfying me or, worse, it is turning me off. If I say 'Please don't do that,' he gets his feelings hurt. And sometimes he gets up and leaves the bed. This is his way of controlling me. There is no room for criticism. Sometimes he stops what he's doing, but the next time he does the same thing again. I keep thinking, This man's intelligent. He has an incredible memory. And yet he can't remember that this turns me off.

Then I think, "Why doesn't he listen to me?" When he doesn't do what I want him to do, I go passive. I lie in bed like a lump. So the two of us struggle for control of how our sex life is going to be.

We struggle for control in a lot of areas. The other day I was raking the leaves. He comes over and tells me I shouldn't be raking them left to right, I should be raking them right to left. Then he takes the rake out of my hand and shows me how to do it. I got mad and went into the house and left him with all the leaves. Then he comes in after me and asks, "Aren't you going to help?" I said, "I don't do it right."

He was out of town for a week. When he came home, he went to the refrigerator to get something to eat. He stood there looking around and then he said, "I can't believe these half-rotten oranges are still in here." Supposedly he was making the comment to himself, but it was obvious that he was making it to me.

I said, "You know where the garbage disposal is. If you think those oranges need to be thrown away, throw them away." He then looked at me and said, "But that's your role." I didn't respond. But I also let them sit in the refrigerator for another week.

We have a lot of roses. I say, "I'm going out to cut the roses." As I'm going out the door, he says, "Here, give me the shears. I'll show you where to cut them." We go over to the cutting bed and he tells me how I should cut them. And while I'm at it, he tells me that I should probably weed. At that point I'm ready to kill him.

Another thing, he always manages to empty the ice cube trays and refill them when I'm at the sink preparing dinner. I'm supposed to stop what I'm doing, step back, let him fill four ice cube trays, and then go on with my work. He thinks he has done me an enormous favor by filling the trays. Last time I said, "I'm in the middle of chopping onions. When I'm finished, you can fill the trays." He said, "That's all right. When you're finished, you can fill the trays."

One of the biggest control problems we have is over our houseplants. My husband thinks the more water you give a plant, the better. When we first got married, I'd go around and water the plants. He'd come home and say, "These plants are dry. Haven't you watered them?" He'd give me a lecture on how plants die if they aren't watered. Then I'd give him a lecture on root rot.

How do I control Luke? Hmm . . . well, if I don't want to do something he suggests, I simply don't answer him. I ignore him. I also change the subject on him. He might say, "Let's go look at cars tonight." And I'll say, "What time do you want to eat dinner?"

A lot of times I'll listen to what he says, and then I'll go do what I want to do. He'll say, "Let's turn the heat down." And then he turns it down. As soon as he's out of the room, I turn it up. I do the same with the air conditioning.

When we don't have these power struggles and things are going well, sex comes easy for us, and there is a lot more regularity. I like that.

Beyond Continuing the Power Struggle

It's understandable why sex for this couple can range in frequency from several times a week to once a month. It's all those power struggles that they take to bed with them that interfere with their sex life.

It's apparent that Luke likes to tell Abby what to do. It sounds as though he is a Corrector. He tells her how to rake the leaves, how to cut the roses, and what her role is supposed to be in the marriage.

It is equally apparent, however, that Abby does not like to be told what to do. When Luke tries to tell her what to do, she turns rebellious and does what she pleases. She is the Passive Aggressive in the relationship.

For instance, when Luke told her about the leaves, she simply went into the house and refused to do anything more. There were certainly more options than taking the power struggle into the house. Abby could have used a little humor, thrown some leaves on Luke and joshed him about telling her how to rake leaves.

When Luke commented about the oranges, instead of telling Luke that he knew where the garbage disposal was and then escalating the power struggle by leaving the oranges in the refrigerator for another week, Abby might have said nicely, "Throw them away." And if Luke didn't throw them away, she could have stopped the power struggle by throwing them away herself.

When Luke doesn't do what she wants him to do sexually, instead of becoming passive, Abby could take his hand and show him again what she wants. Or she could tell him again.

Perhaps Abby sums it up best for every couple when she says, "When we don't have these power struggles and things are going well, sex comes easy for us, and there is a lot more regularity."

ಈ LETTING GO OF THE FIGHT

Perhaps you recognize that you and your mate are like some of the couples in this chapter and that you, too, like to have the last word and your own way. Here are some additional techniques you can use to disengage from those power struggles.

One cognitive technique is the "Peace on Earth—Let It Begin with Me" method. If, for example, your husband insists on showing you how to do something that you already know how to do, you can decide to stand there and listen for the sake of peace—not always, but sometimes.

If he tells you that he thinks you were out of line the other evening when you told everyone at the party how much you paid for a piece of artwork, you can simply say, "I don't agree" and then let it go. If he comes back with the comment, "Well, I think you were wrong to tell everyone," you can say, "Let's agree to disagree." The trick is not to make a big deal out of every issue.

Although I don't think it's healthy to avoid disagreements as a matter of course, there are many struggles for power that can be avoided altogether, and others you can choose to let go of faster. In the end, you'll have a much better relationship and more physical intimacy.

In the novel *Love In The Time Of Cholera*, by Gabriel Garcia Marquez, there is a brief episode in which Dr. Urbino accuses his wife of not having soap in the bath. On being confronted, his wife remembers that her husband is right. But she is annoyed and indignant that he dared point out something that she had not done, so she pretends that there *was* soap in the bath. Because his wife refuses to admit that she is wrong, Dr. Urbino moves out of the bedroom.

For three months he sleeps in the study and the two of them refuse to speak to one another.

Then one night as Dr. Urbino lies on their bed reading and waiting for his wife to finish in the bath, he falls asleep.

When his wife comes out of the bath, she awakens her husband and reminds him that he is supposed to sleep in the study.

> But it felt so comfortable to be back in his great-grandparents' featherbed that he preferred to capitulate.
> "Let me stay," he said. "There was soap."[*]

I have shared this story with many of the couples I see in therapy, and when they get into a power struggle that neither of them will let go of, I ask, "Was there soap?"

This translates, of course, as, "Do you want to stay married, have a good relationship, and make love? Or would you rather continue the fight?"

---

[*] From *Love In The Time Of Cholera* by Gabriel Garcia Marquez, published by Alfred A. Knopf Co. All rights reserved. Reprinted by permission.

CHAPTER SEVEN

TOO LITTLE ATTENTION
OUTSIDE THE BEDROOM

During a therapy session a woman will often complain that she does not feel taken care of in her marriage. As we talk, the woman readily admits that her husband buys her nice gifts and rarely complains about her spending. He never forgets her birthday, and he remembers Valentine's Day. On a day-to-day basis, however, something is missing. Although she can't quite put her finger on it, she feels neglected. In other words, she rarely feels she is the center of his attention.

In the last few years I've seen a number of men with similar complaints. The man believes that his wife loves him, yet he feels that, on some basic level, his wife is not particularly attuned to him.

More specific criticisms regarding lack of attention from one's partner include the following:

"It seems like she would rather talk on the telephone with one of her friends than sit and talk with me."

"My wife has never approached me for sex. Although she rarely turns me down, it would be nice if she took the initiative. It would mean a lot, like she cared."

"Recently I had to see the doctor for a growth on my face. Before the appointment I felt extremely anxious. I already had myself dead and buried. But do you think for a minute my husband could bring himself to ask how my appointment went? Three days I waited before I blasted him for not asking about my face. And do you know what his excuse was? He was waiting for me to bring it up."

"Although I've asked him a million times, never once has he said he loves me without my saying I love him first. I'm quite sure he loves me. What I don't understand is his unwillingness to say so. You'd swear I was asking him to jump off the Empire State Building."

❧ COMPETITION FOR WHO GETS THE ATTENTION

Being unwilling to sit and talk with your partner, refusing to approach your partner sexually, not asking your mate what the doctor had to say, refusing to be the one to first say "I love you": all these complaints are examples of how one partner consciously or subconsciously withholds attention from the other. And when there is not a reciprocal exchange of attention and affection, sex becomes infrequent.

If you do not feel emotionally taken care of in a marriage, you're not going to be very responsive when your partner approaches you for sex. And as time goes on, you will be hesitant to approach your partner, since he or she hasn't responded to your request for other kinds of attention.

In addition to directly withholding attention from one another, many couples subtly compete for attention.

Take the husband who starts to tell his wife about a presentation he made at work that day. The telephone rings. The wife leaves to answer it. A few minutes later she comes back and starts talking about something that happened to her that day. In essence, this wife has shifted the conversation from what her husband was talking about to what she wants to talk about. She becomes the center of attention.

Another example is the man who says to his wife, "How would you like to make love to me tonight?" This question makes him the center of attention. To make his wife the center of attention he would need to say, "I'd like to make love to you tonight. How about it?"

Then there is the case of me and my husband, who fly to Boston for a weekend for a few days of R & R. We get to the hotel and he orders room service, wine, and cheese. I change into a new negligee. He pours me a glass of wine, we toast, and I start to walk across the room. Two steps later, I get my big toe caught in the hem of the negligee. I, along with the wine glass, fly through the air. Wine splashes everywhere and I come crashing to the floor, sure that I have broken something, at least.

My husband looks at me and the first thing he says is, "What are you trying to do, kill yourself?"

With this question my husband was asking me to focus on him and reassure him that I was okay. What I needed was for him to rush to my aid, see if I was hurt, and help me from the floor.

Since this incident took place, whenever I interrupt him when he's talking, which is a way to get the attention focused on me, he says, jokingly, "What are you trying to do, kill yourself?" If, on the other hand, he doesn't answer me when I ask him a question, and I'm kept waiting, which is his way to keep the attention focused on himself, I say, "What are you trying to do, kill yourself?"

We don't do this in front of friends, of course, but privately it has become a playful way to point out that one of us is trying to shift the attention away from the other.

Whose Feelings Get Focused On . . . His or Hers?

A good deal of competition also goes on over who has the right to express feelings and whose feelings count the most.

A wife will get angry over something her husband has done. Instead of him addressing her anger and his behavior, which has irritated her, the husband himself becomes angry. At the end of their argument, she backs down because he has become more angry than she is. He has shifted the focus away from what she feels annoyed about to what he feels annoyed about.

Not too long ago this very dynamic was played out between a couple who are friends of mine. They were having a barbecue with a large number of people. They were serving salsiccia, a kind of sausage.

That morning the wife had grilled about fifty salsiccia herself. She had left the grill for a minute and the sausages caught fire. She salvaged most of them, but when it came time for her husband to grill the other fifty, she warned him not to leave the grill for a moment.

Well, the man failed to heed his wife's warning. He left the grill unattended, and the sausages went up in a blaze. When the fire was out, the wife wagged her pointer finger at her husband and said, "I told you not to leave the grill."

The husband, feeling somewhat irritated, responded, "Well, if you think you're going to ruin my day, I'm not going to let you."

With this statement this husband shifted the attention away from his wife and her feelings to him and his feelings.

Here is another way in which couples use their feelings to compete for attention. The wife feels sad and starts to cry. The husband gets mad or sulks because "he can't stand it when his wife cries." She starts to feel guilty, dries her tears, and reassures him that she'll be okay. He has used his feelings to manipulate the attention away from her and onto himself.

A similar scenario is one where the wife feels sad and down in the dumps. Instead of attending to her feelings, her husband withdraws and pouts because she is not emotionally available for him. His pouting is a way to get the attention away from her and onto himself.

❧ MATES . . . AT STALEMATE

In the following interview you will see a number of competitive maneuvers used by Allison and Clay, who have been married almost twelve years. You will also see how their competitiveness with each other has drastically interfered with their sex life.

This is Allison's second marriage and Clay's first. She is 42; he is 46.

Allison's Side

Since the beginning of our marriage, we have had sex only once or twice a year.

I know that's startling. Clay was shy and embarrassed about sex and I was much more experienced. He didn't know about kissing, or foreplay, or how to use his hands. He worried about keeping his erection, his penile performance. What hurt was that I didn't think he desired me, he didn't focus on me when we had sex. I could have been a Kleenex box.

We had more of a sex life before we got married. Shortly after getting married, Clay was no longer interested. Clay wanted a child. After we had our daughter, sex pretty much stopped.

One night when I approached him, he said, "You're going to have to leave me alone." The mistake I made was to take him at his word and leave him alone. And because he wouldn't approach me, we didn't have sex. Once in awhile he would approach me if he had too much to drink. Naturally, that made me furious.

When I was single, I had a lot of sex and I loved it. It was a time of great sexual freedom. I had lots of fellows, lots of sexual experiences. I went from a lot of sex to almost no sex in a matter of months.

Clay and I used to have horrible fights because I couldn't stand not having sex. I would be frantic. It wasn't because I needed the sexual release so much as it was that I needed the attention. I could relieve myself with a vibrator. What I wanted was to be held, to feel human contact, to feel like a beautiful woman.

If Clay could not perform sexually because of a physical reason, I would understand. He could approach me, hold me, do all the foreplay things and I would use a vibrator. I would have physical release, but more importantly I would have the loving.

Our fights, which sometimes lasted a whole weekend, got us nowhere. Sex is what we fought about. But I know the real issue has always been attention. I think not having sex with me is just another way Clay withholds attention and love.

If I'm sick, Clay becomes angry. If I'm feeling down or anxious, he'll go to his office. He refuses to stay home and take care of me. He gives me financial support but not emotional support.

When we go out, I want to be treated like a woman. I want to be on a date. He wants to be treated like a little boy.

For example, we went to the movies. We had seen part of the picture the week before. When we came to the part we had already seen, Clay looked at me and said, "Are we going to leave now?" When he asked that question, he became a little boy. He doesn't say what he wants. He expects me to make the decision. He expects me to take care of him.

Recently we were on our way to the symphony. He said, "What is the best way to get to Powell Hall?" I told him. When we got to the turnoff, I pointed out the sign. He said, "What do you want me to do now?" Then he said, "I don't know where I am. Do I turn here?" By the time we got to Powell, I felt like I was out with an infant. It's not like we never go to the symphony. Then he got into the parking lot and said, "I don't know where to park."

How can I have sexual feelings for someone who acts like a little boy?

We have had several sexual encounters recently that were good. I approached him and he responded. I now know he will respond if I approach him.

Clay's Side

I don't have as strong a need to have sex as she does. A lot of times it's not worth the effort. She is totally passive in lovemaking, and that's a put-down to me. She just lies there. I have to do everything. She says that I don't perform very well. She can't have an orgasm with me.

The motivation to have sex in the beginning was to have a baby. I wanted a child badly. We kept track of when she was fertile and made a point of making love then. When she got pregnant, the motivation for me was gone.

I've never been able to bring her to orgasm. I bring a vibrator to her. I get the extension cord, plug it in, and lay it on the bed beside her. Generally we have intercourse, I come, and then she uses a vibrator. Years ago I volunteered to use a vibrator on her. She said I was too clumsy. She could tell where the vibrator works best.

When I think back to my early twenties, I had sex about every other weekend. I had plenty of opportunities. But I just didn't pursue it. Sex wasn't that high of a priority.

I want a woman to be the aggressor and I want to be passive. When we got married, Allison was active in the lovemaking and I was passive. She would have oral sex on me. Then one night I told her to leave me alone. I guess I just didn't want to have sex that night.

After that fateful night, nothing much happened.

Very recently, in the last three months, our sex life has started up again. Allison has become more active in bed. She has started approaching me again.

Allison is always saying she wants me to stand up like a man and argue with her. But if I have an opposite viewpoint from her, she throws a fit. You can't have a contrary opinion. When we're not fighting she will admit that she makes mistakes. But while we're arguing, I've never seen her back down or heard her admit to a mistake.

I don't feel comfortable complaining to her about a problem on my job because she always turns the situation around so that it's my fault or else the person who caused the problem should be fired. It's always a half hour of analysis. I don't think she listens to my feelings.

She does not know how to end a conversation. The other night was a good example. A woman had come to the house to drop off some papers. This woman was standing at the door with her hand on the doorknob. Every time she tried to get away, Allison brought up another subject. It took the poor woman 40 minutes to get out the door.

Allison complains that her mother doesn't listen to her, but I hear Allison talking and talking. She won't let her mother get off the phone. Finally her mother will hang up on her.

Allison has something wrong with her almost every morning. She is hypersensitive to all her body functions. Most of the time she thinks she has cancer. If she coughs, it's cancer of the lungs. She has a medical term for everything. She goes to the MERCK Manual and looks up all her symptoms. Then she diagnoses herself. She is into wanting a lot of attention. And I'm not a good attention giver.

The Competition Goes On

Although these are both bright, intelligent people, neither Allison nor Clay is a good attention giver. In fact, each of them compete for the attention in the marriage. Many of their behaviors are subconsciously designed to get and keep the attention focused on themselves.

Clay will not approach Allison sexually. When you approach someone for sex, you make them, for that moment, the center of your attention. Clay refuses to make Allison the center of his attention.

On the other hand, Allison has been reluctant to approach Clay. Yes, Clay did tell Allison not to touch him some years ago, but if Allison really wanted sex, she would have taken the risk and initiated sex again. The way she chose to pursue Clay was by fighting with him over the fact that he didn't pursue her.

According to Clay, on the few occasions when they do have sex, Allison becomes passive. Her passivity in sex is another way to keep the attention focused on her. If Allison's perception is accurate, Clay focuses on his erection, which is a way to keep the attention on himself.

Allison has also never had an orgasm with Clay. Allison's refusal to let Clay use the vibrator on her might be interpreted as a way to shut Clay out and keep the attention solely on herself.

When Allison gets sick or down and needs attention, Clay flees the house so he does not have to give Allison attention.

Allison keeps the attention focused on herself by continually fretting about her body and physical ailments, and by talking on and on, often dominating the conversations in which she participates.

Clay tries to keep the attention focused on himself by not making decisions, such as when to leave the movie or where to park the car. It becomes Allison's responsibility to make the decisions and take care of him.

Because neither Allison nor Clay has been willing to approach the other sexually, thereby recognizing and giving attention to the other, their sex life has been almost nonexistent.

ⅇ "I USE SEX AS A TOOL TO GET AFFECTION"

This next interview illustrates how one man has been having a great deal of sex, over a period of many years, as a way to get his wife's attention.

Pete's Story

I guess we have sex three or four times a week, sometimes more. This has been going on for over twenty years. Angie didn't enjoy sex much in the first five years, but with practice, practice, practice . . . she enjoys it now.

I approach Angie about eighty percent of the time. I approach her with kisses and touching. When she approaches me, she puts on a sexy negligee. This is her way of saying, "I want to make love."

I think we have a lot of sex because Angie doesn't give me attention in other ways. I use sex as a tool to get affection. My wife is just not one to give affection or compliments. I'm the one who gives the compliments in our marriage.

I think sex has actually kept us together. Physically, Angie is a great lover. She has a great body. She always turns me on. But when I look at our marriage outside of bed, it's not very good. Angie is very critical and sarcastic. She is always putting me down about something. I feel she is not my best friend.

When we get dressed up to go out, she says, "How do I look? Do you like what I'm wearing?" She's always concerned about how she looks, but she never tells me how nice I look.

Every time we have sex, it's like she's grading me. She says, "It was great" or "It was so-so." When she says it's great, it's like the act was great, but not necessarily with me.

Sometimes she says, "Why did you come so fast?" or "Why did you slow down?" If I lose my erection, she says, "What's wrong with you?" I think she actually counts how many times I can penetrate her without having an orgasm.

After we have intercourse, she doesn't want to talk. It's like, "Thank you—good night."

Sometimes after sex I feel down. I think, "What am I doing in this marriage? Why do I go to bed with this lady?" She takes care of me physically, but she sure doesn't take care of me emotionally.

I keep having sex hoping that one day she'll recognize that I'm a nice guy, that one day she'll say nice things to me.

Most of Her Attention Is Negative . . .
Even During Sex

Unlike most individuals who withdraw sexually from their mate when they are not being taken care of emotionally, Pete uses sex as a maneuver to get attention. And certainly sex is an important way both to give and to get attention.

But since Pete's wife is critical during sex, in the end he does not feel emotionally taken care of. The attention he gets is negative.

Although Pete says, "I think sex has actually kept us together," one wonders how long the physical pleasures of sex can keep this marriage going.

For a couple to have a good relationship and a healthy, satisfying sex life, each partner needs to feel emotionally taken care of and fulfilled, in and out of bed. This means that it is the responsibility of each partner to make the other, at least some of the time, the center of attention.

𝕰 THREE PLUS THREE EQUALS SEX

One way you can immediately make your partner the center of attention is to give him or her a hug, a pat on the back, a snuggle, or a compliment. Make a pact with yourself to give your partner three strokes a day.

In addition, decide to do three nice things for your mate each day. Bring her coffee in the morning. Drop off her dress at the cleaners. Give him a back rub. Send him a card. Do an extra chore around the house. Pick up her favorite dessert. Offer to fix her a glass of tea when you fix one for yourself.

Another must for a healthy relationship and a healthy sex life is to talk with your partner and really listen. It's so rare for people to let their mate talk without interrupting, or analyzing, or changing the subject, or jumping up and moving on to another chore that must be done that day. If you want to feel close and intimate and have a healthy sex life, you must spend time talking and listening to each other.

Also, don't forget to ask how an important meeting went, or what the doctor had to say, or how a particular project is coming along. Your making a point of keeping in tune with what your partner is doing will make him or her feel special.

When you make your mate feel special, you create an emotional bond between the two of you. Once this emotional bond is there, sexual intimacy will follow.

CHAPTER EIGHT

INHIBITED SEXUAL DESIRE

How does a couple cope when a husband is impotent and cannot maintain enough of an erection to have intercourse? How does a woman's inability to achieve orgasm affect a couple's sex life? What does a couple do when, as soon as she touches his penis, he ejaculates? What happens to one's sex life when, no matter what the wife does, the husband is just not interested in having sex?

An estimated 10 percent of our population suffers from some type of sexual dysfunction. In almost all cases, the sexual dysfunction reduces sexual frequency.

In this chapter you will learn how a sexual dysfunction affects sexual frequency, how dysfunctions affect partners' feelings for each other, how different couples deal with these problems, and what, if anything, one partner can do to keep sex alive in the relationship.

❧ THE MAN WHO SWITCHED OFF

Meet Marc and Suzanne. They have been married for nine years; they lived together for almost two years before marriage. He is forty, she is thirty-four. They have two young children. For both, this is their first marriage. They make love perhaps four times a year.

Marc's Side

A major source of conflict has been our sex life, or lack thereof. Sex was good for the first six months, but after that, sex became less and less frequent. By the time we got married, we had lousy sex. It was almost as though someone threw a switch and turned off any desire I had. As far as I know, absolutely nothing happened between us. I simply no longer desired sex.

Neither of us is satisfied with our sex life, but at this point Suzanne doesn't even want it. My lack of caring about sex, turning her down, the infrequency—with all this I've destroyed her interest in it. We used to fight about my lack of desire. Now my wife doesn't say much about it. Because I have been so unresponsive, Suzanne no longer approaches me.

I think Suzanne's whole attitude about me is influenced by how she feels about me sexually. Since I haven't been there for her, it's like she doesn't respect me. Our relationship was better when we had regular sex. Suzanne was warmer, more affectionate, and more giving. She paid more attention to me. She was more tactile.

For me, I'm not sure how much bearing sex has on how I feel about Suzanne. But our lack of sex certainly affects how Suzanne feels about me.

Suzanne used to get mad at me. Sometimes she would break down and cry. At that time my sexual desire would increase a small amount. Although we wouldn't have sex, I would hold her.

Our lack of sex is entirely my problem. There is absolutely nothing she can do. It's nothing she does. It's me. I have a low sex drive. I just don't desire sex. I don't even think about it! I think my lack of desire is also a product of performance. I am a premature ejaculator. When we do have sex, I will ejaculate before we can have intercourse. I can't control myself. This doesn't bother me, but it does bother Suzanne.

We've tried the squeeze technique, where Suzanne applies pressure to my penis to control my ejaculation. It wasn't a pleasant experience, so we stopped it. After I ejaculated I would apologize, but I wouldn't masturbate her or take care of her. Basically I do not like to touch her genitally.

As a kid I was fearful of sex. It may have been because my older sister was sexually active as a teenager. She had a bad reputation and that hurt my family a lot. She hung around with a fast crowd. My parents constantly fought about my sister. I also would hear guys talking about her. I decided I was not going to be that kind of person. I was not going to have sexual contact with a girl and bring her and my family shame.

I grew up in a kind of tenement situation, and physically I never felt I could hold my own. I'd avoid getting into fights, because if I did, I always got the shit beat out of me.

I never felt like I was acceptable. I used to feel that if someone befriended me, it was out of sympathy for me. Intellectually I never felt equal. I was always in the brightest class at school. But I couldn't bring myself to compete. Also, I was self-conscious about my big nose.

On looking back I think I was depressed as a little kid. I didn't have much joy in my life.

My parents rarely showed any affection for each other. My mother was very depressed when I was a child. I remember her constantly crying. I think Mom was frustrated because we always had financial problems. She also felt my father was more loyal to his parents than he was to her. I think my dad just kind of ignored her.

I always said I would never have a marriage like my parents'. And here I am. We don't have much intimacy, sexually or any other way. My wife is depressed about it. And I basically ignore her.

Suzanne's Side

Marc has a lot of good qualities. He is intelligent. Everyone loves him. When we met I could sit and talk about problems I was having and he would listen. He was very affectionate. He gave me lots of attention. I loved him. We did things I enjoy doing. Marc seemed at ease with other people. He could fit into a lot of different environments.

From the beginning, sex was an issue because I was disappointed. He would immediately ejaculate and then not bring me to orgasm. He has always been concerned about his own sexual pleasure. When the relationship began, I would get pleasure out of giving pleasure to Marc.

In the ten years that we have been together, I think my feelings about sex have changed. I no longer see intercourse as the big pie in the sky. When we have sex, Marc participates somewhat in my orgasm. He touches me a little and I masturbate. I don't think he's particularly turned on by masturbating me. He's not turned on by my body. Nothing that I know of turns him on. When he gets the idea that he wants to have sex, he gets turned on. I don't approach him because he always turns me down.

There have been some years when we haven't had sex at all. I really felt rejected. But I never thought the problem was mine. In a previous relationship sex was so good that I didn't go into this marriage doubting my own sexuality.

About six years ago Marc and I went to a sex therapist for a year. We were struggling with the question of whether to have children. Marc didn't know if he wanted children. We also focused on our sex life. Sex got a little better, but the therapy did not have a lasting effect.

Sex has not been an issue that has been pushed underground. At the same time I'm worn down. And at this point I'm not doing anything about it.

Yes, I masturbate. How else could I get by?

I don't think sex is a central issue in my life anymore. A few years ago I would have said, "I will have an affair when the kids get older and I don't have as many obligations." Now I say, "I won't have an affair."

I'm not sure if I have changed, if I have settled into a pattern of almost no sex, or if it's the fear of AIDS. Sex doesn't turn me on like it used to. It may also be that I have small children at home—I'm always running after them and I'm tired.

Inhibited Sexual Desire: What Can This Couple Do?

Clinically, Marc is suffering from what has been termed *inhibited sexual desire* (ISD). This means that he has little or no sexual activity and that the desire for sex is simply not there. Marc and Suzanne have sex infrequently, and Marc does not think about sex or fantasize about it. Nothing his wife does or doesn't do seems to have any impact.

It is estimated that twenty to forty percent of people suffer from ISD at some time in their life. Usually the cause is a result of a major life change, such as loss of a job or the death of a parent. ISD may also be a result of depression, drug abuse, alcoholism, or marital discord. A hormone deficiency, the onset of diabetes, and pituitary tumors also may cause lack of desire.

Unfortunately for Marc and Suzanne, Marc's lack of desire has been a lifelong issue. Even as an adolescent he avoided sex.

Current thinking in the field suggests that a lifetime of ISD may be the result of an inability to be close to another person. It may result from a poor self-image or from performance anxiety.

Certainly Marc has a number of adversities that might cause lack of desire. He had an unhappy childhood. He did not witness nor experience closeness in his nuclear family. And he suffered and still suffers from a poor self-image.

Marc is also a premature ejaculator, a condition that he thinks causes his lack of desire. This may be true, because ISD often develops as a means of dealing with a preexisting sexual dysfunction. If Marc can subconsciously block out any desire for sex, he doesn't have to deal with the fact that he is a premature ejaculator.

It's curious that Marc sees his lack of desire as his problem alone. Clearly this is Suzanne's problem, too. Unless Suzanne goes outside of her marriage for sex, she must suppress her desire or continue to feel unhappy and frustrated.

Unlike many people whose partners do not desire sex, Suzanne does not see Marc's lack of desire as a reflection on her. As she herself points out, "I didn't go into this marriage doubting my sexuality."

One does wonder, however, why Suzanne decided to marry Marc, when it was clear almost from the beginning of their relationship that he was not particularly interested in sex. Perhaps she discounted the importance of sex in marriage. Perhaps she thought Marc would change and eventually become more interested in sex. Perhaps she herself fears closeness and Marc's lack of desire unconsciously serves her as well.

What is clear is that Marc and Suzanne's entire relationship is suffering from their lack of sexual contact. This couple needs to get back into therapy. By Suzanne's own admission, their previous work with a sex therapist made sex somewhat better, perhaps because they were forced to address the problem on a regular basis and so felt obligated to have sex.

Another must is for Marc to have a complete physical examination to rule out any physical problem that may be causing his lack of desire.

Marc might also get into some individual therapy or group therapy where he could deal with his sexual problems, his early childhood issues, and his poor self-image.

Suzanne, too, might consider therapy to explore why she was willing to settle for a marriage that she knew would have sexual problems—and why she has been willing to go along with an almost sexless relationship.

Another possibility is for this couple to get into marriage counseling together. The marriage counselor should be one who deals not only with relationship problems but with sexual issues.

The important thing is that this couple get help *immediately* and stop being passive about this problem that is clearly eating away at their marriage.

≈ "HE WILL NEVER BE ABLE TO PUT HIS IMPOTENCE BEHIND HIM"

For the first time in their seven years of marriage, Michael (41) and Stacy (33) are now physically able to have intercourse. Instead of sex enhancing the marriage, however, it has brought serious problems to the relationship.

Michael and Stacy Tell Their Story

Michael: I met Stacy in May of 1979. From the beginning, I felt tremendously attracted to her looks, her personality, and her athletic skills. Stacy was perfect. We had great times doing things together.

Stacey: We tried to have sex when we were dating, but Michael could not get an erection. He was totally impotent. Michael had been married previously and had never had problems sexually. He thought something must be wrong with him physically. In fact, he was adamant that his inability to have an erection was the result of something physical. He simply did not desire sex. Nor did he feel sexual at any time.

We enjoyed each other in so many ways that we decided to get married despite Michael's impotence. Before we got married, Michael expressed a concern about my being deprived of a sexual relationship. I said, "I can take it or leave it." I was 26 and had not been very active sexually. The first time I had sex, I had gotten pregnant and had an abortion. So I was reluctant to enjoy sex. In fact, I avoided it in most situations.

Right before we got married, Michael saw an internist who said his impotence was probably the result of the stress of a new relationship and told him that "these things sometimes happen." He gave Michael an injection of vitamin B-12, but it didn't help.

So he went back to his internist, who then referred him to a urologist. The urologist ran a number of tests and said he didn't see anything wrong. Michael once again returned to his internist, who sent him to another urologist.

Michael: Both urologists gave me a physical and did blood work. They tested my testosterone level and did a urinalysis, but found nothing unusual. Because no one found anything physically wrong, my internist suggested that I see a psychiatrist.

I went to the psychiatrist three times. Stacy saw him once. In the first two sessions he took my life history. Then he gave me a psychological test. He said that I was a classic case of an impotent male. He recommended that I meet with him twice a week and also attend a therapy group.

Stacy: The psychiatrist told Michael that it would take approximately two to three years to solve the problem. With this information, Michael decided not to return. I supported him in his decision.

Invariably when Michael and I had intimate times together, sitting on the couch and talking, we wound up talking about sex. We believed this was the only thing lacking in our relationship. When I would say that something must be wrong with me to step into this kind of a marriage and that I must need counseling in the area of my sexuality, Michael would say, "It's not you, it's me."

Early on he made attempts to masturbate me, but I found it awkward and embarrassing. I was exposing myself; he needed nothing from me.

Michael: Then came the fall of '85. I was driving to the office when I became nauseous and began to sweat. I had hot and cold flashes. It was a bright day and I had some sensitivity to the light. I felt increasingly sick. When I got to the office, I shut my door and lay down. I then went to the infirmary. I had them turn the lights out. I couldn't stand the lights. I was sweating unbelievably. The doctor examined me and checked my vital signs. He said it appeared that I had the flu. He told me to go home and sleep it off. I went home and slept until 2:00 that afternoon. When I got up I felt fine. That night I played racquetball.

A year later, I was driving to work and the same thing happened. I got to work and lay down for awhile. Then I called Stacy and said, "I'm coming home. I've got that same flu I had last year."

I got on the highway and I thought I was going to die. I had a tremendous pain behind my eyes. I could feel my pulse racing. I put my head down on the steering wheel. I pulled off the highway and drove down the shoulder. I stopped the car and was violently sick to my stomach. I was sweating profusely. The pain was right behind my eyes. I prayed for someone to stop and help me. Finally I managed to start driving again. I drove directly to the hospital emergency room.

The doctor there ordered a CAT scan, which revealed a tumor resting against my pituitary gland. It had caused part of the gland to deteriorate. Based on the size of the tumor, the doctors determined that I had had it for at least fifteen years. They also found that it was prolactin secreting, which meant the tumor was not malignant and would respond to medication.

The doctor said, "I am going to make you better than you have ever been. You don't realize how bad you've been feeling. Your male hormones are going to come back. You are going to become more aggressive. Your sexual function will return. The biggest problem is that you will need to adjust to these changes; it would be a good idea to get some counseling."

In September I began taking the drug to eradicate the tumor. My sexual function returned in January. Stacy and I had intercourse. We were both ecstatic.

Stacy: We had long talks about our need to develop an ongoing sexual relationship with each other, and just how we were going to go about doing that. By that time we had lived together for seven years.

Michael: I didn't view her as a sexual partner. We had lived together too long in a nonsexual way.

Stacy: I was dealing with my own insecurity about my sexuality. Things just didn't reverse themselves for me. No one gave me a magic pill. I was just not that interested in sex. On the other hand, Michael wanted sex. He loved his renewed sexual powers as well as his new personality. He became more assertive and less easygoing. He started to have a temper. He felt that he was a man again. He became obsessed with his weight, his clothes, his hair.

About four months after Michael was able to have sex, I became aware that he was having an affair. I came home from a trip and smelled perfume on the sheets. I was humiliated that he and some woman could come to our house and flaunt this in front of me.

When I confronted Michael about having an affair, he denied it. But I knew.

Michael and I are still living together, but I think I'm too much a reminder of his impotence. He will never be able to put his impotence behind him as long as I'm around. Sex has absolutely ruined our relationship.

Michael: Regarding the future of the marriage, I think the relationship will not make it. I'll probably get out. I have no doubt that if I had not gotten well, we would be together. It's unfair. Stacy has not changed. I have. I feel uncomfortable for her. But I like the new me.

Was It Sex That Ruined This Relationship?

In this marriage both partners suffered from ISD. In Michael's case his lack of desire, as well as his impotence, was the result of a pituitary tumor. Stacy's lack of desire, on the other hand, seems to be psychological in origin. Consider her own assessment that she could "take it (sex) or leave it," and the fact that she did not view herself as very interested in sex.

Because Michael had apparently resigned himself to not having sex and Stacy wasn't particularly interested in it, lack of sex did not seem to have a strong adverse effect on the marriage. As soon as Michael regained his ability to have sex, however, Stacy's lack of desire became a major problem. Besides, as Michael said, "I didn't view her as a sexual partner. We had lived together too long in a non-sexual way."

Perhaps if Michael had given Stacy more time to adjust to his renewed manhood, she would have been able to tap into her own sexuality. As she said, "No one gave me a magic pill," referring both to Michael's reawakened sexual interest and to her own lack of interest.

Michael's new personality also added to the strain that was suddenly put on the marriage. In four short months Michael became more assertive and less easygoing. He was more interested in his looks, his clothes, and his body. Suddenly Stacy had to relate to a husband who seemed to have returned to an earlier time in life and was once again experiencing the excitement and passion of adolescence.

Was it sex that ruined this relationship? Or was it because sex was never a part of the relationship? Was it another woman, or was it, as Stacy said, that "I'm too much a reminder of his impotence"?

One internist and two urologists missed the tumor on Michael's pituitary gland, although the signs pointed to a physical problem. Michael had had no sexual problems with his first wife and then became completely impotent. It is well-documented medically that a lack of sexual desire, as well as impotence, may be the result of a pituitary tumor. In fact, ten to twenty percent of men with ISD have pituitary tumors that produce excessive amounts of prolactin, a hormone that suppresses testosterone production.

Perhaps this story will give others the determination to follow their own instincts and persist in seeking yet another medical opinion if they suspect that their sexual problem is physical.

❧ "I THINK OF SEX AS CHOCOLATE ICE CREAM OR CORN ON THE COB . . . IT'S GOOD NOW AND THEN"

Bob and Kate have been married for fifteen months and are already having problems with sex. Both are in their late twenties.

Kate's Side:

My husband won't approach me for sex. He doesn't seem interested. Normally we have sex every six to eight weeks. Now I'm trying to get pregnant, so it's on the increase; but it's a struggle to get Bob interested, even when our goal is to have a child.

I have a hard time initiating sex because I think Bob doesn't want me. If he would approach me sometimes, I would feel attractive and sexy. Because he doesn't approach me, I have started to feel shy and embarrassed about approaching him.

Bob and I met about two and a half years ago. It took him two or three weeks just to kiss me. But I thought, Here is a man who will talk to me, a man I don't always have to fight off. At the time his nonpushiness appealed to me. It was kind of pleasant. Then, about three months into the relationship, Bob proposed. He proposed every day until I accepted.

We had sex before we got married, maybe every week to week and a half. At that time Bob definitely took the initiative. We also did a lot of cuddling and snuggling without sex. About a year after we met, we moved in together. Sex got less and less frequent after that.

I didn't complain about our sex life because we were so busy that I never understood there was a problem. We had a large wedding, so we had a lot of preparations. But I realize now we definitely have a problem!

I can be stark naked, walk into the room, pull Bob down on the bed, and he doesn't react. He is not aroused by my body. The longer he goes without initiating, the angrier I get. I want him to pursue me. I want to feel sexy. Other men have told me I have nice legs, a nice tush, but not Bob. I had a long relationship with one man, and we had sex every time we met. It never dawned on me that I wouldn't have much sex in my marriage.

If we have sex, I do the approaching. I blow in his ear, I caress him. I play with the hairs on his chest. I work my way down. He lies there. He puts his hands over his head. I get no response except maybe a groan. This lets me know that what I'm doing is wonderful, but I get nothing back. If I keep fooling around with him, he comes, and that's that. I get nothing.

I've learned to stop at a certain point. He doesn't get any more foreplay until he gives me some. When I stop, he masturbates me. Always he goes for the gold . . . my vagina and clitoris. I get very little stimulation on other parts of my body. He never kisses me. He doesn't caress my breasts. He doesn't nibble my neck. He waits for me to climax. I think he enjoys it when I climax. It's almost like he roots me on. He says, "Come on, you can do it." After I come, we have intercourse and then he comes.

When I do initiate sex, he doesn't reject me. But I'm always the one who has to start the whole lovemaking process.

Bob's Side:

I've never been an overly sexual person. During college I didn't date much, so I didn't have much sex. I fantasize about sex on a limited basis. I don't look at a girl and think about sex with her. I never talk about sex. If the mood strikes me, I'll approach Kate. But it rarely ever does. If I had to choose how much sex I might like to have, I would have it every couple of months.

I don't think there is anything wrong with me. I enjoy sex. I don't have trouble having an erection. I don't have trouble having orgasm. Sometimes I have the opposite problem. I need to slow down a bit. I usually ejaculate within three or four minutes of having intercourse.

Kate wants me to approach her. She uses her anger to try to get me to approach her, as opposed to just approaching me. She thinks my not approaching means that I don't care about her. It's not that I don't care. It's just that sex is not that important to me. I guess maybe I could adjust to more sex for the sake of Kate and our marriage.

There is nothing that bothers me about Kate. If she were to dress differently or act differently, that wouldn't change anything. I guess the one thing she could do is to get off my back about sex.

I masturbate, but rarely. I was brought up to believe masturbation was dirty. Nice people didn't do it. In fact, nice people probably didn't have sex. I've always assumed my mother and father only had sex twice, once to get pregnant with me and once to get pregnant with my sister.

I think of sex as chocolate ice cream or corn on the cob. It's good now and then. It isn't a necessity for me to be happy. I don't feel frustrated if I don't have sex.

There Is a Solution — If Kate Will Use It

Although Bob doesn't feel frustrated if he doesn't have sex, Kate feels very frustrated and unhappy because Bob is not particularly interested.

One can only speculate as to Bob's lack of interest. Perhaps it's because he carries a belief from childhood that sex is dirty and nice people don't engage in such activity. It may be that Bob's testosterone level is low.

Some clinicians would say that Bob is indeed suffering from ISD. Others would say that he simply has a lower sex drive than most people; and if it's not a problem for him, it's not a problem. Everyone would agree, however, that Bob's low sex drive *does* create a relationship problem.

The one thing I question is Kate's denial that she didn't realize that there was a sex problem before marriage. No matter how busy a couple is, they almost always find the time for sex, particularly when a relationship is new.

I suspect that Kate fell in love with Bob, and she was aware that her biological clock was ticking. If she had looked too closely at the relationship and started questioning Bob's lack of sexual desire, she might have been forced to question her decision to get married. This decision might have ultimately led to her giving up any chance of having a child. So she put her knowledge about Bob's lack of desire aside and conveniently blamed it on their busy schedules.

The one saving factor is that Bob will have sex with Kate if she does the approaching. Therefore, if Kate can get through her embarrassment and bad feelings about always needing to be the aggressor, this couple could have sex more frequently. And maybe Bob would come to be more interested in sex and start approaching Kate, since, as he said, "I guess I could adjust to more sex for the sake of Kate and our marriage."

❧ GO TO A MARRIAGE COUNSELOR . . . A SEX CLINIC . . . DO SOMETHING!

If you are not having sex as frequently as you would like and you have reason to believe the cause is a physical or psychological problem that is directly related to sex, go to a marriage counselor who deals with sexual disorders; or go to a sex clinic; or start with your physician. But do something. Don't wait for the problem to magically go away, because it won't. Also, the longer you let the problem drag on, the harder it will be to erase the bad feelings that will build up because of the lack of sex in your relationship. If you face a serious roadblock that requires professional help, make a pact with yourself now to take action by the end of this week.

CHAPTER NINE

CHILDREN—HOW THEY INTERFERE WITH SEX

Couples almost always report that after they have a child, sexual frequency goes down. On a good day an infant takes an estimated nine hours of care. That's sixty-three additional hours of work per week! It's no wonder, then, that new parents feel exhausted and have little time for each other. It is this lack of time, as well as sheer tiredness, that leads to less sex after baby arrives.

Since both parents often work outside the home, it's not long before questions come up. Whose responsibility is it to find a baby sitter for the child? Who will drive the child to day care? Who bathes the child and puts her to bed at night? What time should she go to bed? Who watches her on Saturday?

I've worked with couples who sought marriage counseling because the man no longer felt important after the birth of their child. I've seen women in therapy who felt resentful because their husbands demanded they work outside the home, while these women want to stay home and take care of the baby. Also, because many husbands still expect their wives to take most of the responsibility for child care and do most of the housework, women often feel cheated and trapped.

As a child gets older, many parents clash over how the child should be reared. What should they require the child to do around the house? Whose responsibility is it to lay out the chores and then lay down the law when the child doesn't do them? How much money should they allow a child to spend on a pair of tennis shoes? If the child gets poor grades, or gets in trouble with drugs, or develops a smart-mouth, whose fault is it?

Once a couple has children, sex usually becomes less frequent because they have less time to focus on each other and less energy because of increased responsibilities—and because power struggles arise over how the child should be handled.

If a couple has more than one child, they are going to have less time and more problems.

❧ THE WOMAN WHO COULDN'T MAKE LOVE TO A TASKMASTER

Now meet Ed and Beth. In their early forties, they have been married for nineteen years. They have three children ages eighteen, fourteen, and twelve.

Beth's Story

Some months we have sex once a week. But mostly it's only once every few weeks. I feel close to Ed when we have sex. I think he feels that way too.

I think we would have sex more if we weren't so tired. We both work, and work takes a lot of our energy.

Sometimes Ed has to go out of town on business. He travels about ten days every month. Also, we don't make love when I have my period.

Sometimes Ed doesn't have the most romantic approach. He might just touch my genitals, and then want to have intercourse. Sometimes I turn him down when he does that. I'd rather go a little more slowly—talk, kiss, hug. I like to be hugged. It gives me a sense of security. When I tell Ed this, he says, "I'm not your father."

I think the biggest reason that I'm not willing to make love more is that I get angry with Ed. It's usually about the way he has handled one of the children. If he approaches me when I'm angry, I turn over and say, "I'm too tired." Sometimes I'm honest and say, "I can't make love with you; I don't like the way you handled the children tonight."

My husband gets irritated and angry with the boys a lot. He continually fights with our oldest son, Scott, and there is a lot of tension in the house. I can't relax enough to feel loving when this happens.

Ed gets angry about Scott's room being messy. He gets mad at him for spending too much time in the bathroom. In the morning we all have to leave about the same time, and we only have one bathroom. Scott could be faster, but I don't think it's unusual for a teenager to take a lot of time in the bathroom.

Sunday morning is a problem. We go to church. Scott is always late, and the whole family has to wait for him. I remember I used to be like that too. Everyone had to wait for me. My husband doesn't like to be late, so he gets angry and then he calls our son names. He says, "You're such a jerk. You're stupid. I wish you'd get out of this house." The other day he said, "I wish you'd never been born." I tell Ed that's not the way to approach Scott. If he would just talk to him instead of always telling him what to do. . . .

Ed thinks that an eighteen year old should be self-sufficient, that he should know what he wants to do in life and not rely on his parents for emotional support. He also thinks Scott should earn most of his own money.

Ed is rigid. He has his ideas of how a family and household should be run. He has an idea about what everyone's role should be—how I should act, what my duties are. He expects me to take most of the responsibility for the children, organizing their schedules, making sure everything gets done for them. Occasionally he takes them to a soccer game. He thinks I shouldn't buy anything for the kids unless they really, really need it. His idea of what they need and my idea of what they need are different. He thinks children should keep their rooms neat. They should put everything back in its place. He doesn't like it when their friends come over and make a lot of noise. I often defend the kids against my husband. Sometimes I think I'm too permissive with the kids. But Ed's too strict.

Ed demands a lot of me and the children, but he doesn't give much positive reinforcement for what we do accomplish. I also don't think he shows his love enough. He seems to have trouble showing affection after a child becomes an adolescent. Once you're an adolescent, the hugs stop. I think he sees showing affection as a weakness.

His parents died when he was very young and he was raised in an orphanage. Everything was run by the clock. They had to get up and go to bed at a certain time. They ate at a certain time, and probably they didn't have a choice about what they ate. I guess that's why Ed expects a lot of self-discipline from his family.

Funny thing, though, Ed will often sit in front of the television for hours and not do anything himself. But that's probably good. He needs to relax.

Ed uses the money he makes as a way to control us. He says, "I earn most of the money, so I'm the boss." When he goes out of town, he doesn't give me the checkbook, which is his way to discourage me from spending. I get around him, though, by going to the bank and getting a check from the teller.

Part of our problem is that there is not a lot of money. Ed thinks we could live more simply. I really don't think we could. We are middle class; our kids expect certain things, such as being able to participate in sports. I want to be able to give them that. Ed had to work for everything when he was a child, so he expects our children to earn everything they have. I came from a middle-class background, and my parents gave me things. Ed thinks I'm spoiled. I don't think so.

Strangely, though, I love him. I like his strength of character. Family means a lot to him, and I respect that about him. He has a really cute sense of humor. He fits my idea of masculinity.

It's all very complicated, isn't it? I want him to be strong and decisive, and I want someone I can lean on, someone who makes decisions and makes me feel secure. But I also want him to be sensitive, to give me understanding and affection, to let me be independent and make my own decisions.

Maybe we should be more tolerant of each other. We are healthy. We are doing the best we can. If Ed would just discuss things with the children instead of always getting angry with them. Ed sees fatherhood as being the boss, not being a friend and confidant. I see a parent's role as more nurturing. Maybe we balance each other out. He provides the expectations. I provide the nurturing. What we need is to work more together.

Mom Rescues, Dad Persecutes

It seems that, despite the conflicts in this marriage, Beth genuinely loves Ed. The problems that she keeps running into concern their children. And it is these problems that interfere most with this couple's sex life.

It's easy to see that Beth is more accepting of the children's behavior—whereas Ed is more demanding and critical. Beth is the Caretaker and Ed is the Corrector. Beth thinks the children need nurturing and emotional support. Ed views this as "babying" them.

In this family Beth tends to play Rescuer to her children. This means that she not only accepts their inappropriate behavior but she makes excuses for it. An example of this is when she says in the interview, "Scott is always late, and the whole family has to wait for him." But then she excuses his behavior by adding, "I remember I used to be like that too."

What Beth fails to see is that Scott is persecuting the family by making everyone wait. Scott's lateness is a way to be rebellious and persecute Dad, who "doesn't like to be late." Beth chooses to focus on Ed's inappropriate name-calling of Scott, rather than Scott's provocative behavior. By continually rescuing her son, Beth inadvertently invites Ed to persecute him. For whenever you have one parent who always takes the role of the good guy, the stage is set for the other parent to take the role of the bad guy.

What would be helpful here would be for Beth to stop defending the children. She could also discipline them more often. Ed, too, could change the dynamics in the family by backing off and not always assuming the role of the disciplinarian. This would at least set the stage for Beth to discipline the children more.

Another thing that influences how Ed and Beth handle their children is the way they themselves were raised. Ed believes his children should be raised as he was, with a lot of rules and little nurturing. Beth, on the other hand, came from a more accepting, giving, and supportive environment, and she wants her children to have the same experience.

Although their children do not keep this couple from having sex, the disagreements they have over the children certainly create enough tension and negative feelings between the two of them to ensure that their sex life is not as good as it could be.

❧ A TEST: ARE YOUR CHILDREN UNDERMINING YOUR SEX LIFE?

In order to become more introspective about whether your children or stepchildren are a source of negative feelings between you and your mate—enough so as to interfere with your sex life—take the following test. Answer each question with a yes or no response. You may want to pencil your answers into the margin.

1. Do you frequently get into arguments with your partner over value-laden issues, such as what movies the children should be allowed to see . . . how much money they should spend . . . what toys they should be allowed to have . . . how many chores they

should be required to do . . . what time they should go to bed?

2. Have you confided in your child things that you do not like about your mate or arguments that you are presently having with your partner, thus trying to win your child over to your way of thinking?

3. Do you find yourself using such excuses as "The children will hear us," or "The baby will be awake any minute," in order to avoid sex with your mate?

4. Do you and your mate disagree about school issues and how homework should be handled?

5. If your mate has told your child no, do you often reverse the decision and let your child do what he or she wants?

6. Do you often give so much time and energy to the children that you have little time and energy left over for your mate?

7. If your partner and your child get into an argument, do you often take your child's side, overtly or covertly?

8. Does one of you do more than 65 percent of the parenting chores—running the children to lessons, attending P.T.A. meetings, helping with homework, clothes shopping, disciplining, tucking them into bed at night?

9. Do you and your mate fight over such issues as how little time he gives to the children . . . how much you pamper them . . . whether he is too critical with them . . . how you're always on their case about something?

10. If your mate corrects your child, do you butt in and recorrect the child, thereby undermining your mate's authority?

11. Do you operate from the position that you almost always know better than your mate what is right for your child?

12. Do you feel as though your children get the lion's share of attention from your mate while you go almost unnoticed?

13. Do you frequently feel resentful toward your mate because of the money that gets spent on the children for clothes, entertainment, education?

14. Have you gone to bed angry with your mate any time in the last seven days as a result of a disagreement over a child?

15. Do your children see the two of you as divided most of the time on issues that concern them?

If you have three or more yes answers, you are allowing your children to create distance between you and your mate, and your sex life is suffering as a result.

❧ GOOD PARENTS HAVE BETTER SEX LIVES

Keep in mind that children can be a wonderful asset to your relationship. They can give you a multitude of things to talk about, an incredible number of things to worry about, a number of things to weep about, and certainly a great many things to laugh about.

If you respect each other as parents and keep in mind that you're in it together, trying to raise your children to be good people, your children will indeed provide an additional avenue for closeness and physical intimacy.

CHAPTER TEN

MORE REASONS FOR LITTLE OR NO SEX

On any given night there are a variety of factors that can prevent a couple from having sex. Perhaps they are exhausted from working, or he needs to finish writing a report, or she has to get up early to catch a flight, or he's down in the dumps about his business. Throughout marriage these factors, along with the underlying issues that have already been addressed, can contribute to a lack of sex, as you will read in the next three interviews.

❧ THE BEDROOM STAND-OFF

Lisa and Phil, who have been married for fourteen years, are in their late thirties and have a two-year-old child.

Phil and Lisa Tell Their Story

Lisa: We might have sex once a month, but it can be less often than that. Sometimes we go for periods of six or seven weeks. If we haven't had sex in a long time, there is an awkwardness there, like, "What should we do first?"

We were both virgins when we got married. In the beginning Phil complained about not having enough sex and the quality of our sex. I think he thought other people had sex all the time. He would bring home sex manuals for me to read. He would highlight passages in certain chapters. That made me feel very inadequate. He would say I needed to experiment. He wanted me to be the aggressor.

I'm the one stuck with getting things done in our relationship. If Phil does something, it's because I've specifically told him to do it. If I want work done on the house, I call the repairman. I get the estimates. It's my feeling that I do a lot more than he does. He thinks he does more than I give him credit for. I refuse to take the responsibility for sex because it makes me feel like it's just another job. I think he should be the one to initiate sex.

Sometimes I'm angry at Phil, and that interferes with sex. When I'm pissed off, I don't feel like being close to him.

For example, when I woke up the other morning, I saw three items that he hadn't taken care of that he said he'd do. A bag of clothes was sitting in the living room that he had agreed to return to the store three months ago. The wastebasket was overflowing. He had thrown his dirty clothes on top of a basket of clean laundry. When I complained about his dirty clothes, he used the excuse that there wasn't a hook on the back of the door for him to hang them on. I said that he'd had four years to put a hook on the back of that door!

Phil: I think a major reason we don't have sex more has to do with how busy we are. It seems that we should make sex a higher priority and put it above the demands of work and home. But those demands are more pressing, and, if unattended, they create immediate problems.

If I have a report due at work, it's due, no ifs, ands, or buts about it. I have to pay bills by a certain date. If I don't pay a bill, I'm going to hear about it immediately. Whereas if we don't have sex, there is no immediate problem.

Lisa: The way we live, things get done by calamity. I get home from work late. I start dinner. We get our son to bed. I do laundry so we have underwear. By that time it's nine o'clock. Then it's pay bills and give each other a brief rundown of what's happened during the day. Everything seems to have immediacy but sex.

We also tend not to go to bed together. Phil stays up late. He reads, does paperwork, and watches movies. This is how he unwinds. I go to bed earlier than he does because I'm exhausted. To some extent I think our going to bed at different times is an avoidance of sex.

Phil: Another issue is that if you get in the habit of not having a lot of sex, it's easy to maintain that pattern. That's our pattern—infrequent sex.

Then there's the friction between us. I may be in the mood for an intimate evening. Then Lisa comes home and complains about something I did or didn't do. This ruins the evening, and any attempt at intimacy would be a waste of time.

Lisa: Our sex life has been warped by infertility. For years I tried to get pregnant. I have endometriosis. Phil has a high sperm count but low motility.

We used to take my temperature every morning before I got out of bed. We had days when we were supposed to abstain from sex. Then we had optimum days when we were supposed to have sex for eight to ten days in a row. That was probably the most often we have ever had it.

We were told to have sex with Phil on top and a
pillow underneath my fanny so I slanted downward. He
couldn't withdraw for a half-hour, then I had to lie there
for an hour afterwards.

Since then we've had everything from artificial insemination in the doctor's office to artificial insemination
at home where Phil put the semen inside of me with a
syringe. Sex was business. We were having sex to have
a child. We were not having sex for pleasure.

Phil: I wanted a child with my genes. I was hung
up on the notion of my family being carried on geneti-
cally, so I wanted us to try every single medical option
available. I did not want to adopt unless I was sure we
couldn't have a biological child.

Lisa had three special operations to try to correct
her infertility problems. Then we tried in vitro fertiliza-
tion. When that failed, it was like a death.

While Lisa was being treated for her infertility problem, I was being treated for mine. I took a number of
different medications to change my hormonal levels to
help the sperm swim better and stay alive. The medications had side effects, such as fatty deposits in my
breasts and the hair that grew on my earlobes.

One of the worst things for me was the sperm test.
It's embarrassing giving a sample in a doctor's office.
They put me in a small room with no lock on the door.
I could hear people walking by and talking in the next
room. The cup they give you for the sample looks like
one that you get a milkshake in. I remember thinking,
"I'm supposed to fill this up? If everyone else can fill
this up, no wonder I have a problem." Every time I
walked out with the sample, I felt like people were
looking at me to see how red I was.

As it turned out, eventually we adopted. Adopting
a child was one of the most wonderful things that
happened to us. It's hard for me to fathom that I could
have a genetic baby more wonderful than he is.

Lisa: We used to have sex in the morning. Our son changed our routine. We refer to him as our human alarm clock.

There are times when sex is very painful for me because of the endometriosis. It's like Spanish moss inside my body. Now I have a growth on one of my ovaries. It also grows on my tubes, the outside of my uterus, my bladder, and my colon. Because penetration is sometimes painful, you kind of lose the spontaneity.

Phil: I think our lack of sex also stems from my wife's traditional notion that men should initiate. So if I don't initiate, there is a very good chance we're not going to have it.

Lisa: Well, it's my personal feeling that men don't have the big sex drive that they claim they do. When I talk to other women, they say, "We haven't had sex in so long." One of my friends who recently married said, "I don't think I'm an unreasonable woman. I would like sex at least once a week, but he just doesn't seem interested."

Sometimes when Phil approaches me I think it's out of obligation. At the same time, after we have sex we both say, "Gosh, that was great. We should do that more often." Sometimes I enjoy what we refer to as a quickie. When we haven't had sex for a long time, it gets us back into it.

Phil: When we have sex, it helps us get through a lot of problems. It's much better for us as a couple. It makes us intimate in a way that nothing else does. It's like it reinforces an invisible bond, and then when we have problems, they are easier to weather.

Frequency Takes a Nose Dive

Probably the main thing that has caused sex to become infrequent in this marriage is that both Phil and Lisa want the other to do the approaching, and both have an elaborate rationale for their own position.

Phil contends that their lack of sex is the result of Lisa's traditional notion that men should initiate sex. Because she doesn't initiate, they don't have sex very often. On the other hand, Lisa's rationale for not approaching Phil is that she feels she already does more than her fair share in this marriage. And when both partners wait for the other to do the approaching, sex is not likely to happen.

It also seems that neither of them feels comfortable with experimenting sexually. Phil certainly made his own timidity known when he brought Lisa highlighted pages from sex manuals. Again, it seems that Phil sees it as Lisa's responsibility to take the lead sexually and to be more experimental and playful.

Anger also plays a part. The interview indicates that Lisa is a Caretaker. (Note her comment, "I'm the one stuck with getting things done in the relationship.") Phil, on the other hand, is a Passive Aggressive; when Phil doesn't do what he has agreed to do, the result is that Lisa feels irritated and is not likely to want to make love.

Fertility problems have also put a strain on this couple's sex life. As with most couples who experience infertility, sex became a task with a goal, and sometimes even a burden, instead of an expression of love and intimacy. Physical pain because of endometriosis also puts a damper on desiring and enjoying sex.

Certainly being tired plays a role, too. Both partners are professionals with heavy schedules, and they have an active two year old who rarely sleeps late enough to allow them to have sex in the morning.

Put Sex on Your List of Things to Do

What Phil and Lisa need to do is make sex a priority. They might set aside one night a week for sex. After their son is in bed, they should get in bed, talk, and make love. Or they might hire a baby sitter to take their son out every Saturday afternoon while they stay home and get intimate. Unfortunately, in this busy world we live in, sex sometimes needs to appear as an item on our list of things to do.

Another way for Phil and Lisa to improve their sex lives significantly is for each of them to make the decision to approach the other. They might agree that from the first to the fifteenth of a given month, Lisa will be the initiator. From the fifteenth to the thirtieth, Phil will initiate. This agreement would get both of them out of the power struggle over who is to initiate sex and into the habit of taking responsibility and initiating it.

❧ "ONE DAY I SAID, 'REMEMBER SEX?' "

Meet Deedee, aged 32, and Alan, aged 33. They have been married for seven years, and at present they have sex less than once a month.

Deedee's Side:

In the beginning we had sex about two or three times a week. We were sexually active about a year before we married. That frequency continued two or three years into our marriage. Then we were separated for about five months because of Alan's job. That broke our pattern. When we got back together, sex dropped to once a week or once every other week. That frequency probably lasted about two years.

I got pregnant. If we had intercourse, I'd have contractions. The doctor said it was something in Alan's sperm that caused the contractions, so we stopped sex altogether. We didn't do oral sex or masturbate or anything. I wasn't interested in sex, and Alan wasn't interested in the alternatives.

Then I had Jessie. She's now three. While I was nursing, I felt awkward about sex. My breasts were so big, and I thought they had a different function. They were for the nourishment of our baby, not for sexual stimulation.

I returned to work when Jessie was six weeks old. I wanted to work, but Alan also expected me to work. We had to get up with the baby in the middle of the night, and I was tired. Probably a whole year went by when we abstained, somewhere from my fourth month of pregnancy to about six months after she was born.

One day we sat down and I said, "Remember sex? I like it. Let's do that again." I think we have made incredible progress. We're up to once a month. I would like to have sex once or twice a week, but I don't pursue it.

Actually, I think about sex a lot, but it's usually when Alan's not around, before he gets home from work, or in the evening when he's out running errands. When he's at home, the thought of having sex sort of evaporates. I don't know why I don't think about it when he's around. Maybe it's because he's not very affectionate. It's like he waits for me to give him affection as opposed to him giving me affection.

Early in our marriage we had more time. Now we need to wait until Jessie is in bed. Or we have to wake up before she does. Or we wait until she's with her grandparents. I think knowing that "tonight's the night" puts more pressure on us. It gives the act too much significance, because it's the only time we can do it. For me this makes it less enjoyable.

Sometimes I don't enjoy sex because Alan occasionally can't come. He always has an erection. There's never any problem getting him excited. He just can't ejaculate. It's a huge frustration for me and for him. I think that's why he doesn't approach me more often. He used to get angry with me when that happened. Now he doesn't show his anger, but I think he still sees it as my fault, somehow.

When we were first married, Alan went to work and came home after eight hours. Now, instead of him just having a job, he has a career. He used to initiate sex a lot, and he used to get on me about bringing my work home. It took me several years to get my job under control so that I didn't work all day and four hours every night. Now our roles have switched and I'm the one who says, "Cut that out. No more working at home."

When I was single, I might have been able to talk about this sort of thing with my roommate. But Alan is my roommate now, and I don't think I can talk to him about it without him getting defensive. I can talk to other women about problems at work or problems in my marriage, but not about why we are not having sex.

Alan's Side:

I think we got into this once-a-month pattern because it was difficult to have sex when Deedee was pregnant. Then the responsibility of raising Jessie changed our lives, and sex took a back seat. Deedee's going after a master's degree also has had an impact. My career, with each job change, seems to get more and more involved. The weeks are totally filled, Monday through Friday. On the weekend we concentrate on Jessie, and there doesn't seem to be any time left over for us. Before Jessie was born, we were able to take our time and have sex on Saturday or Sunday morning. Now she wakes up early and it's not possible.

Most of the time I approach Deedee. She rarely turns me down. I snuggle up to her and kiss her on the neck and she snuggles back. If I see that she's getting turned on, then I'm turned on.

I think I don't approach her more because of her anger. I say to myself, "She's too angry." I would rather go to sleep than try to talk through what's bothering her so we can have sex. She is angry at me because I don't do things around the house that she expects me to do. I don't think the things she wants me to do necessarily need to be done—for instance, picking up my clothes and throwing them down the chute. I throw them next to it. Hey, I'm piling them there so I can throw them all down at once.

I think housework should always be hired out. And if that can't happen, I would rather live in a dirty house than a clean house where we're at each other's throats. Deedee came from a family where her grandmother and mother were very concerned with having a clean house. I came from a family where it was acceptable to let things slide. Our house wasn't filthy, but it wasn't spotless.

Deedee is always badgering me to help her with the housework. When the house is clean she is happy. She has what she wants. But I'm angry. In addition, if we clean the house for two or three hours on a Saturday, when that's done I have to go outside and cut the grass. It's like I can start doing my chores only after I finish helping with hers.

I also resist when she adds something new to my list. This makes her angry. But if I concede and do what she wants, this makes me angry. It's sort of like we play a game of Ping-Pong, except it's with anger.

Another example of why she gets angry: my not folding the clothes after she washes them. That's our agreement. To me it's no big deal to go to the laundry basket and pick up a clean pair of underwear.

Another thing that makes her angry is that I always seem to run about fifteen minutes late. In her mind, if I say I'll be home at 6:00, it means 6:00. In my mind it means 6:00, give or take twenty minutes.

I think the main reason I don't approach her is that I don't really feel taken care of by her. She just doesn't seem interested in my life. I'm not the most important thing to her. I feel like I'm third or fourth. First is her job, and then our daughter, and then how the house looks, and then me, trailing behind. I think she likes me, but there isn't a burning love.

When I completed my master's degree or got promotions at work, there was no recognition. She didn't jump up and down and give me praise. She never gave me a gift or a card. Nothing.

I think one of the ways people can take care of each other is by being flexible. It seems that when I need her to be flexible, she makes it very painful. Instead of saying, "Yes, I understand that you have to work late," she acts as if I'm doing it to spite her. I guess she's mad because she feels like she's not being taken care of.

Occasionally I enjoy her wearing sexy lingerie. It turns me on, and we have better sex. She's become more resistant to that recently. We talked about the lingerie, and she said she thought I was fantasizing about someone else. I said it emphasized her body, and I thought she looked sexy. We agreed she would wear special lingerie when I asked her, but I wouldn't ask her every time. It would really be nice, though, if she would wear it for me sometimes and I wouldn't have to ask.

It seems like our marriage is a lot of negotiating and bargaining for position. It's "I'll do these things if you do those things." Neither of us is likely to do additional things such as offer to drop off the other person's cleaning or go to the store to pick up something the other person needs.

Our relationship is a lot different than my parents' relationship. My dad worked and my mom stayed home. My dad was the ruler of the house. What he said went. Everyone had to live by his rules, including my mom.

My parents showed a lot of affection when I was young. This left me with the impression that they were truly in love. That was very comforting to me. It also left me with the impression that we had a very stable family.

In my relationship with Deedee, I see us more as partners with equal say. What I don't see is the affection between us, and I miss that. It was my fantasy that your wife would hug you, and kiss you, and shower you with affection.

Not Special . . . Not Courted . . . Not Generous

Alan and Deedee's marriage is almost a perfect reflection of the struggles that many young married professionals are facing today. Both of them are well educated. They have demanding careers that call for more than forty hours of work per week. They have a small child, a house to care for, and little time for sex.

It's clear that Alan expects Deedee to pull her weight financially. This is true with most young couples today. Men expect women to work outside the home regardless of children. In return, Deedee expects Alan to do his share around the house.

The problem, however, is that although Alan says that he sees himself and Deedee "as partners with equal say," he resents the equality. Intellectually he understands that they need to share chores, but emotionally he cannot accept the fact that he should do housework. He thinks "housework should always be hired out," and he talks about "helping" Deedee, which shows whose responsibility he thinks housework is. This position is congruent with that of many educated men. Studies have shown that the more educated a man, the more he resents and resists doing housework. Alan resists by throwing his clothes on the floor instead of down the clothes chute and by not keeping his agreement to fold the laundry.

In response to Alan's not keeping his bargains, Deedee gets angry. In response to Deedee's anger, Alan does not approach her for sex.

Another problem is that Deedee and Alan have different standards of acceptable cleanliness. As Alan noted, "Deedee came from a family where her grandmother and mother were very concerned with having a clean house. I came from a family where it was acceptable to let things slide."

As with Phil and Lisa, the last couple we looked at, Alan and Deedee believe that the demands of a small child and lack of time in general play a role in their lack of sex.

As for Alan's occasional inability to ejaculate, one can only speculate on the cause. It may be because he is overly tired or he has some unresolved anger for Deedee; or he may be overly sensitive to Deedee's anger.

Probably one of the main reasons that Alan and Deedee do not make love more often is that neither of them feels special or courted or taken care of by the other. There seems to be a lack of generosity on their parts.

Deedee's perception is that she is not being taken care of. Alan's perception, on the other hand, is that Deedee does not see him as special. In his eyes, she puts her job, their daughter, and the house before him.

Hire a Housekeeper . . .
Wear a Sexy Nightgown . . .
Approach Her

This couple could do several things immediately that would make each of them feel more loving toward the other.

What Alan could do is start keeping his word. If he agrees to do something, then he should do it. Or he should say up front that he is not willing to do a particular chore, such as folding the laundry. Better to say he is not willing to do something than to agree to do it and then not follow through.

What Deedee might do is to lower her standards of housekeeping, hire household help, or decide that if the house is to meet her standards, she is probably going to be the one who will do more of the housework. It seems futile, however, for her to keep expecting and demanding that Alan accept her standards. It sounds as though Deedee's anger is not effective in getting Alan to change. What's more, it is killing any affection she feels for him, and it is killing his affection for her.

What is most evident is that both Alan and Deedee need to take better care of each other. Alan might make a special point of giving Deedee a hug each night when he walks in the door. He might tell her how terrific she looks. He could volunteer to do something around the house that he knows would please her, and he could approach her more for sex. After all, she's not angry every night.

Deedee could decide to wear a sexy nightgown more often. She might offer to give Alan a backrub, bring him a small surprise each week, and also approach him for sex.

It's evident that if Deedee and Alan made only a few of these changes, there would be more intimacy in this marriage.

⅋ "INTERCOURSE HAS BECOME A BIG, LOOMING PROBLEM"

If you think Job from the Bible had troubles, read about the next couple. Rita (37) and Jack (40) have had to deal with an infertility problem, a possibility of testicular cancer, periodic bouts of depression and anger, premature ejaculation, *and* the fear of intimacy.

Rita and Alex Tell Their Story

Rita: We have sex two, maybe three, times a year. And those times are when we're on vacation. Usually all our sex happens over the course of one week. Sex gradually tapered down through the years, and no one complained. We have sort of a fear of getting close. When one of us is making overtures, the other person picks up on the clues and pulls away. If we spend a nice evening together, I set it up that when Alex gets back from taking the baby sitter home, I'm doing something— reading, watching television, folding laundry. If, on the other hand, I put on a sexy nightgown, which signals that I'm interested in making love, it is Alex who turns on the television or starts reading. One of us will change the mood. Since we don't have sex very often, intercourse has become a big, looming problem. So it's less risky not to initiate anything. We have kind of a thin wall that keeps us apart.

Alex: I would like to make love more often. But it's so difficult to do, because we've fallen into a pattern. It requires a real self-conscious change in the way we relate. We'd have to take a risk to get back into sex.

I think we are physically self-conscious. We are no longer trim 30-year-olds. When we had sex in the beginning, Rita was a knockout and I was good-looking, muscular, trim, blond, athletic.

Rita: One thing that has interfered with sex is that Alex has early ejaculation. Within two minutes, if I touch his penis or even his stomach, he ejaculates. We read about the squeeze technique, but that seemed too artificial. When we first married, we had sex a whole lot. By the third time in the evening, Alex wasn't so fast. That's why it wasn't so much of an issue then. But neither of us has that much time or energy now.

At first I was pretty understanding about Alex being a premature ejaculator. Then I started getting mad. I'd physically push him away after he came. I think his fear of rejection is pretty high.

Alex: My premature ejaculation wasn't a problem in the beginning. It was something we laughed about. She would say, "There you go again." I think it bothered me more than it bothered her.

Rita: After he climaxes, he sometimes masturbates me. And it works fine—but sometimes I feel like he gets too mechanical.

Generally, I've been the initiator. If I don't start it, it doesn't happen.

Part of my not being willing to initiate goes back to what I call my "angry phase," a time when it seemed Alex wasn't putting anything into the marriage—when I felt last on his priority list.

I never knew when he was coming home. He would call and say, "I'm on my way," and then not leave his office for another hour. Sometimes he was too busy to get me a birthday or Christmas present. He didn't do things he said he would do, like home repair jobs, getting a will together, helping around the house. He never did dishes, even if I was sick, unless I asked him. He usually didn't get home before 7:00 or 7:30 at night, and frequently he would work Saturday and/or Sunday. I got to feeling like I was always nagging him, which I was. And then he didn't feel that he had to do anything because I was nagging him.

Another reason for not having sex is our inability to conceive a child. When we found out that we couldn't procreate, making love was sort of sad.

Alex: It was a real blow to Rita and me. I had always dreamed of having children, and that dream was shattered. This took a key focus out of our sexual relationship. Both of us had been raised with strong religious training. And even though I have abandoned my religion, the attitude has remained that the purpose of sex was to procreate.

I think we were both sexually repressed people engaging in a good deal of sex because there was a purpose. When children were clearly out of the sex act, it became sex for sex's sake, and I became much more conscious about sex. It was a reminder that it wasn't going to lead to anything.

I also had to have one testicle removed because of the threat of cancer. I then felt less of a man. My testosterone level was reduced, and to some extent my desire diminished. We tried testosterone injections, but that made us feel even more anxious about sex. I didn't like having an injection to make me horny. It just didn't seem natural. Within two months I stopped the injections. I couldn't handle it. I think Rita was irritated because I gave up so quickly. This is when we put sex away.

The urologist who was taking care of me really messed up. He said, "You are totally sterile. There is no chance of having a child. But just in case, you should use birth control." Then he sent us out the door. He did not suggest counseling or discuss alternatives like adoption or artificial insemination. We were not assisted in mourning. When we found out that we couldn't have a child, it was the death of a dream.

My response was to bite the bullet, face the fact that we weren't going to have a child, and move on. Rita's response was to grab that one glimmer of hope. She pressed for sex and talked about the possibility of having a child. Every time she talked about a child, it hurt me. It reopened the wound.

After we learned I was sterile, we eventually agreed to have a child through artificial insemination. At first I resisted, because it sounded so weird. But I'm proud to say Rita pressed ahead and said she would like to take the risk and go through the hassle. So I finally consented. It was the greatest decision of our marriage.

When Rita got pregnant, I spent the first four or five months repressing my joy because of the fear that Rita might lose the child. We had waited for this for nine years.

When our son arrived, I was extremely joyful. I shouted, "It's a boy. It's a beautiful baby boy." I was the happiest father that there ever was. There was never any insecurity. This was my child.

Rita: Another problem we've struggled with throughout the marriage is my depression. At times, it felt like everything I had to do during the day was an effort. The joy pretty much had gone out of my life. After I had the baby, I was no longer a size eight. I was a size twelve. I couldn't fit into my clothes, but I didn't want to buy any more clothes because I thought I'd lose the weight. I wasn't comfortable going out because I didn't have anything to wear. This all added to my depression.

About four years ago I became so depressed and angry because our relationship was so lousy that I decided to go into counseling. I went alone for awhile and then the therapist and I agreed that Alex should come too. He was dragged kicking and screaming into therapy. We went into separate therapy groups. He was very defensive and I was very angry.

What I got from group therapy was a validation— other people saying if their spouse did some of the inconsiderate things that Alex did, they would be angry too. I was also made aware of what I did to keep the situation going, how I bought into his excuses.

I was confronted with how I dealt with my anger. I used to turn into a screaming, raving maniac, and the group helped me realize how futile that behavior was.

Alex was really adept at changing the subject when I brought up what I didn't like. I learned to get my issue heard by saying, "That's not the issue," or "We'll talk about your issue when I'm finished talking about mine." I also learned some techniques for expressing my wants and needs. Since I was in a separate group, I was able to express my anger and rid myself of a lot of negative feelings without hurting Alex.

Then we went into marriage counseling. Now we had a watchdog, so we were good when we came in. We dropped even more of our negative behavior. I dropped my accusing tone, and Alex dropped his defensiveness. We both listened to each other's feelings. We got homework assignments that helped.

Alex got an assignment to initiate conversation three times a day. That one really helped a lot, even though I knew he was counting the times so he could report back to our therapist. We had sex because we were communicating and getting closer. We went out more; we did fun things together.

We did some touching exercises, massage kinds of things. One night one person gets taken care of, and the next night the other person gets taken care of. We started out nonsexually and then moved to a more sexually stimulating massage. This also helped with sex, but we didn't keep it up very long. It seemed artificial.

When we left therapy, our marriage was good and we were having some sex. But soon after, we stopped having sex again. It's easy to get out of the habit.

If I were to describe our relationship now, I think I'd use the word "comfortable." We get along well. Our relationship is amiable. We do a lot of cuddling, a lot of nonsexual hugging. I wouldn't use terms like "wonderful," "exciting," "great." I think adding sex could make it that.

Alex: I can't keep using the excuse that I'm sterile or that I have a decreased testosterone level; I still get horny. Besides, spring is here. It's time we started having sex again.

Postscript: "We Had Sex!"

From this story, it is clear that this couple was on the verge of having sex again. What they needed was for one of them to make a decision, take the risk, and reintroduce sex into their marriage.

About three months after I did the interviews with Rita and Alex, I got a telephone call from Rita. The first thing she said was, "Has that book you're writing gone into print yet?"

I answered that it hadn't, and that I was still working on the project. Then she said, half laughing, "Well, we took the plunge. We had sex. Not once, but three different times. Print that."

Postscript #2: So Did a Lot of Other People

As I reported in the first chapter, a number of people that I interviewed for this book called to tell me that their sex lives had gotten better since their interviews. Once again, my guess is that they started focusing on why they weren't having sex very often. They started thinking about sex a lot more. And soon, they were having more sex.

CHAPTER ELEVEN

GOOD SEX BEGINS
WHILE YOUR CLOTHES ARE STILL ON

Human beings have a wonderful gift: the capacity to change. If you don't like the way your relationship is going or the fact that sex has been put on the back burner, you can do something about it. Tonight you can approach your partner for sex, and chances are he or she will respond positively.

If your mate turns you down, you can use the examples in this book to help you examine your own behavior and see what you need to change—so that your partner won't continue to turn you down.

After you make those changes, you can approach your mate again, and most probably he or she will be willing to make love.

Remember: No one has to live today in the pattern of yesterday.

≈ EXPECT ONLY 20% FROM YOUR MATE

If, in reading this book, you recognized that you are a Caretaker who gives too much energy to your mate, causing you to feel emotionally cheated yourself, you can start meeting more of your own needs and taking a little less care of your partner. This shift in focus will change the dynamics of your relationship, and your partner will start paying more attention to you. When this happens, both of you will feel like making love more often.

It's also good to keep in mind that no one person can meet all your wants and needs. In fact, your partner is probably capable of satisfying only twenty percent of them. For the other eighty percent you will need to look to other family members, to friends, to your job, and to hobbies. And, of course, you will need to look to yourself.

A List of His Good Qualities

You may have discovered that you are a Corrector, or that you have a lot of Corrector tendencies. If so, that's probably why your partner has not been interested in sex with you. You may have pulled away from him, too, because you're so focused on his flaws. Make a decision to look at his good qualities.

One woman said that every time she starts feeling discouraged about what her husband doesn't do, she makes a list of all he does do. After making such a list, she always feels more loving toward him.

Another way to stop making so many critical comments is to keep in mind the following story . . .

The Muddy Road

Once upon a time, two monks, Tanzan and Ekido, were traveling down a muddy road. A heavy rain was falling. As they rounded a bend, they came to a rushing stream. A young woman stood by the stream, afraid to cross it.

"Come on," said Tanzan, "I will help you." Lifting the girl in his arms, he carried her over the water and then bid her farewell.

Later that night when the two monks reached their destination, Ekido could restrain himself no longer. Taking his friend by the arm, he said, "We monks do not go near females, especially young and lovely ones. It is dangerous. Why did you carry the girl to the other bank?"

"Why, I left the girl there hours ago," said Tanzan. "Are you still carrying her?"[*]

Too often we carry criticisms and hurts to bed—when we could easily leave them in the den.

---

[*] From *Zen Flesh, Zen Bones*, by Paul Reps, published by Charles E. Tuttle, Inc. All rights reserved. Reprinted by permission.

Make Two Decisions

If you're the Passive Aggressive member of your household and you're always doing what you darn well please, make two decisions. First, always take your mate into account before you decide to do something. Second, do what you say you're going to do. This will stop a lot of your wife's criticisms, and it will leave the door wide open for a renewed sex life.

Reach Out

If you are passive in the relationship, you can decide to start taking more responsibility. Make a decision to do two new things a day. Your new behavior might be to reach out and give your wife a hug or to make a suggestion, such as going for a walk together. Taking action will make you feel more powerful and will give you the energy to approach your wife sexually. When you take charge some of the time, she will see you as someone who is more interesting to be with and someone she wants to make love with.

Arguing Is Optional

If you find that your everyday life is filled with hassles and quarrels, have the courage to stay on the topic you are discussing without bringing in old hurts and angers. Also have the courage to let a conflict go. Not every issue has to be analyzed and dissected, nor do you have to place blame as to whose fault the argument was in the first place.

So often a couple will be arguing furiously over some topic when the telephone rings. The wife will pick up the telephone, turn on a pleasant voice, and have a nice conversation. A few minutes later she will hang up the receiver, and in an instant the couple will be back arguing again. If people can turn an argument off when necessary, they can leave it turned off and discuss the problem more calmly.

Arguing is optional. The more you argue, the less loving you will feel and the less you will want to have sex.

Giving Your Mate What She Wants

Another important ingredient of a healthy sex life is mutual attention. Give your mate the kind of attention that he or she asks for. If your husband has asked you to wear a sexy nightgown, wear it. If your wife says that she needs to be told that you love her, do it. It's ironic that people frequently ask their mate to make changes and yet they themselves resist changes that their mate has requested.

Sex Takes Time

Spending time together outside of bed is going to bring you closer in bed. Too many couples don't do things socially together and then wonder why they are no longer having sex. Go to a movie, have another couple over for dinner, take a day together to run errands and have lunch. Falling in love, staying in love, and making love require time together.

Keep in mind, too, that you don't always have to be in the mood to have sex. If your partner is in the mood, you can go ahead and respond, and chances are you'll get in the mood.

৵ "I PARADED AROUND THE HOUSE HALF NAKED"

Remember Jerry and Roberta? They were the couple who fought about where he was going to be buried, how late he stayed up at night, how much time she took to market, what temperature the thermostat should be set on . . .

Here is a follow-up interview with Jerry.

Jerry's Change

Last night I took my shirt off and paraded around the house half naked. Son of a gun, what I thought would happen happened. She smiled and said, "If you want sex, get undressed and come over here."

It was a real pleasure! It had been four months since we had sex.

What changed? Me; I changed. A couple of days ago Roberta came home from the beauty parlor and I noticed that she had a different hairstyle. I made a big point of telling her she looked great.

She brought home a new dress. She put it on and I told her how sensational she looked in it. Then she got a new pair of shoes. I said, "Oh, you bought new shoes." I recognized what she had done.

Remember that big storm we had the other day, an inch and a half of rain in an hour? Water was pouring in the back door because the drain couldn't take the water. She said, "If you'd put a bigger drain in there, we wouldn't have this problem." I said nothing. In the past I would have given her a rebuttal such as, "If you want a bigger drain, you come up with the five thousand to pay for it."

Later that night we were going to dinner. I put on my raincoat and took my umbrella. I asked her if she was going to take an umbrella. She said, "No, the parking attendant will have one." Normally I would have said,

"For Pete's sake, take a raincoat or an umbrella! Can't you see it's pouring?" I said nothing.

We had severe storm warnings. She was afraid and asked me to go down to the basement. I went down with her. Of course, I had to bring down the mail and my checkbook and read my monthly statement. You know I have trouble with the idea of wasting time. But normally I wouldn't have been as cooperative or sensitive about her fear of the storm. I might have said, "We're not having a tornado, we're only having a thunderstorm. So relax. We don't need to go to the basement." But this time I didn't!

When she came home yesterday, I asked her if she had any groceries. Then I said, "I'll help you unload them." In the past I would never have volunteered to help.

A friend of mine noticed that one of our light fixtures had a bad wire. I wanted to take the fixture down and have it fixed. She didn't want me to take it down. She thought I might get electrocuted. So I told her to get someone to come in. She made arrangements for an electrician to come to the house. I accepted this willingly, and I didn't give her a hassle about spending the extra money. I didn't insist on having it my way.

You see, I've changed. I decided to do some giving in on some matters. And she decided to have sex with me again.

❧ IT ONLY TAKES ONE PERSON TO CHANGE A RELATIONSHIP

Perhaps this story will be an inspiration to you; it definitely shows that one person can make enough of a difference to bring sex back into the relationship.

And it clearly demonstrates that *"good sex begins while your clothes are still on."*

NOTES

Chapter One

Page 20: Doris Wild Helmering, *Happily Ever After* (New York: Warner Books, Inc., 1986). Updated here, the four personality tests originally appeared in *Happily Ever After*, chapter 9, pp. 117-129.

Page 24: Ibid. For a complete understanding of how someone can come to develop a particular personality, see chapter five, pp.73-108, and chapter 9, pp. 117-147.

Page 26: Anne Morrow Lindbergh, *Gift From The Sea* (New York: Random House, Inc., 1977), p. 56.

Chapter Four

Pages 87-88: Doris Wild Helmering, *Closer Encounters* [video] (St. Louis, Missouri: H, L & L Productions, 1988).

Page 97: Philip Blumstein and Pepper Schwartz, *American Couples: Money, Work, and Sex* (New York: William Morrow, 1983), p. 201.

Chapter Eleven

Page 197: William Masters, Virginia Johnson, Robert C. Kolodny; *Masters and Johnson on Sex And Human Loving*, Second Edition (Boston: Little, Brown, 1985), p. 452.

BIBLIOGRAPHY

American Psychiatric Association. *Diagnostic and Statistical Manual of Mental Disorders, Third Edition, Revised.* Washington, D.C.: American Psychiatric Association, 1987.

Benderly, Beryl Lieff. *The Myth of Two Minds.* New York: Doubleday, 1987.

Black, Claudia. *Repeat After Me.* Denver, Colorado: Mac Publishing, 1985.

Blumstein, Philip, and Schwartz, Pepper. *American Couples: Money, Work, and Sex.* New York: William Morrow, 1983.

Botwin, Carol. *Is There Sex After Marriage?* Boston: Little, Brown, 1985.

Carter, Steven, and Sokol, Julia. *What Really Happens in Bed.* New York: M. Evans and Company, Inc., 1989.

Frank, Ellen, et al. "Frequency of Sexual Dysfunction in 'Normal' Couples." *N. Engl. J. Med.,* 299:199-215, 1978.

Gelman, David, et al. "Not Tonight, Dear." *Newsweek,* 64-66, October 26, 1987.

Goethals, G.W., Steel, R.S., and Broude, G.J. *Theories and Research on Marriage: A Review and Some New Directions.* In Henry Grunebaum and Jacob Christ (eds.) *Contemporary Marriage: Structure, Dynamics and Therapy.* Boston: Little, Brown, 1976.

Haley, Jay. "Marriage Therapy." *Arch. Gen. Psych.,* 8:213-234, March 1963.

— ed. *Changing Families: A Family Therapy Reader.* New York/London: Grune and Stratton, 1971.

— *Uncommon Therapy: The Psychiatric Techniques of Milton H. Erickson, M.D.* New York: W. W. Norton, 1973.

Helmering, Doris Wild. *Happily Ever After.* New York: Warner Books, Inc., 1986.

— *Closer Encounters* (video). St. Louis, Missouri: H, L & L Productions, 1988.

Jackson, Don D. "The Individual and the Larger Contexts," in *General Systems Theory and Psychiatry,* eds. W. Gray et al. Seaside, Cal., Intersystems Publishers, 1982.

Kaplan, Helen Singer. *The New Sex Therapy: Active Treatment of Sexual Dysfunctions*. New York: Brunner/Mazel, 1974, 1981.

— *The Evaluation of Sexual Disorders: Psychological and Medical Aspects*. New York: Brunner/Mazel, 1983.

— *Disorders of Sexual Desire*. New York: Brunner/Mazel, 1979.

— "Do Other Women Enjoy Sex More?" *Redbook*, p. 44, April 1986.

— "I've Stopped Caring About Sex." *Redbook*, p. 86, September 1986.

Kelley, K., ed. *Females, Males, and Sexuality: Theories and Research*. Albany, New York: State University of New York Press, 1987.

Lindbergh, Anne Morrow. *Gift From The Sea*. New York: Random House, Inc., 1977.

Marquez, Gabriel Garcia. *Love In The Time Of Cholera*. New York: Alfred A. Knopf, Inc., 1988.

Masters, William H., and Johnson, Virginia E. *Human Sexual Inadequacy*. Boston: Little, Brown, 1970.

— *Human Sexual Response*. Boston: Little, Brown, 1966.

— Robert C. Kolodny. *Masters and Johnson on Sex and Human Loving*, Second Edition. Boston: Little, Brown, 1985.

NOVA. *The Pinks and the Blues*. Boston: WGBH Transcripts, 1980.

O'Connor, Dagmar. *How to Make Love to the Same Person for the Rest of Your Life and Still Love It*. New York: Doubleday, 1985.

Penney, Alexandra. *Great Sex*. G.P. Putnam's Sons, 1985.

Reps, Paul. *Zen Flesh, Zen Bones*. Vermont: Tuttle & Co., 1958.

Reynolds, David K. *Water Bears No Scars*. New York: William Morrow, 1987.

Scarf, Maggie. *Intimate Partners: Patterns in Love and Marriage*. New York: Random House, Inc., 1987.

Schiff, Jacqui Lee. *Cathexis Reader*. New York: Harper & Row Publishers, Inc., 1975.

Schiff, Aaron Wolfe, and Jacqui Lee Schiff. "Passivity." *Transactional Analysis Journal* 1, no. 1 (January 1971).

Young, Dean, and Drake, Stan. "Blondie." New York: King Features Syndicate, May 21, 1989.

INDEX